Artificial Intelligence: The Download

By

Rafael Fermoselle, Ph.D.

Artificial Intelligence has been weaponized by cybercriminals and hostile states, without ethical or moral considerations, outpacing science fiction, and placing humankind at the border of global annihilation

Artificial Intelligence? The Download

Gotham Books

30 N Gould St.
Ste. 20820, Sheridan, WY 82801
https://gothambooksinc.com/

Phone: 1 (307) 464-7800

© 2023 *Rafael Fermoselle.* All rights reserved.

No part of this book may be reproduced, stored in a retrieval system, or transmitted by any means without the written permission of the author.

Derechos reservados conforme a la ley de derechos de autor
Tous droits réservés en vertu de la loi sur le droit d'auteur

Published by Gotham Books (July 21, 2023)

ISBN: 979-8-88775-386-7 (P)
ISBN: 979-8-88775-387-4 (E)

Because of the dynamic nature of the Internet, any web addresses or links contained in this book may have changed since publication and may no longer be valid.

The views expressed in this work are solely those of the author and do not necessarily reflect the views of the publisher, and the publisher hereby disclaims any responsibility for them.

Weaponizing Artificial Intelligence

Includes Index

1. Fermoselle, Rafael, 1946-
2. Artificial intelligence
3. Weaponizing artificial intelligence
4. Biometrics
5. Cybersecurity
6. Deception
7. Data
8. Biotechnology
9. Cybercriminals
10. Personal privacy
11. Predictive analytics
12. Ransomware
13. Espionage
14. National Security
15. Intelligence community
16. Data integration

TABLE OF CONTENTS

Acknowledgements 8
Executive Summary 9
Résumé 10
Resumen Ejecutivo 11
Introduction 12
What is *Artificial Intelligence* (AI)? 16
Intelligent Automation (IA) 17
Definition of Data 18
    Data Validation, Metrics, and Big Data 18
    Weaponizing 'Big Data' with AI 20
What are Systems? 21
    Systems Theory 21
    System of Systems (SoS) 21
    System validation 23
What are computers? 25
What is Quantum Computing? 28
What are Computer Chips? 29
What are Algorithms? 34
What are Biometrics? 34
    Types of Biometrics 35
    Biometrics Reliability 36
Biotechnology 39
    Medical and Bio-Medical Research 39
    Embedding Chips in Humans 40
What is Social Media? 42
    Social Media and AI 44
    Is "Social Media' Good or Bad? 45
    Social Media is a Warzone 46
Speech Recognition 49
    Speech Recognition Algorithms 50
    Computer-Assisted Translation (CAT) 50

- Computer-Assisted Interpretation vs Simultaneous Translation 51
- Foreign Language '*Converters*' 51
- More Tools for Cyber Criminals 53
  - ChatBot or Chatterbot – What is it? 54
  - ChatGPT -a Godsend or a Hex? 54
  - Microsoft 'Bing' and Google 'Bard' 56
  - Video *Deepfakes* and *Synthetic Media* 57
- Personal Privacy: A Thing of the Past 58
  - Affinity Credit Cards 59
  - Frequent Flyer Programs 60
  - Facial Recognition Technology (FRT) 61
  - Luggage Tags 62
  - Ubiquitous Technical Surveillance (UTS) with AI 63
  - Hyped Brain Wave Monitoring Technology 63
  - Cyber-Exotic Brain-Computer Interface (BCI) 65
  - Mitigation Strategies to Reduce Exposure to Bad Actors 66
- Ransomware Cybercriminals 70
  - Top Ransomware Gangs 71
  - Convicted Russian Cyber Criminals 75
  - Russian Cybercriminals Wanted by the FBI 76
- Online Content Generated by AI by 2025 82
- Autonomous Vehicles and Passenger Planes 83
- Humanoids, *Gynoids, and Fembots* 83
- Predictive Analytics Generated by AI 85
  - Doomsday Predicted by AI 87
  - Doomsday Clock Pushed Closer to Midnight 88
- *Deception*: a Classic Weapon of Intelligence 90
  - AI: a Perfect Tool for Deception 90
  - AI: Multi-Disciplinary Approach for Deception 92
  - AI: Open-Source Intelligence Collection and Analysis 92
- Weaponizing Artificial Intelligence (AI) 95
  - Braggadocio Before the Russian-Ukraine War in 2022 97
    - Weaponized AI Without Arrogance: Israeli Style 97

Russian-Ukraine War	108
Conventional Weapons	109
Ukrainian Weaponized AI	113
Ukraine's AI Companies	116
Russian Hi-Tech Weapons Systems	122
Russian Military Sloppiness	123
Russia Deploys Combat Robots to Fight Tanks	127
Russian Air War Over Ukraine	129
Weaponizing AI: U.S. Experience	130
Efforts to Maintain American Leadership in AI	131
Education in the U.S. is in Crisis	134
Shambolic American Export Controls	136
A Dysfunctional Relationship with China	139
A Chinese Trojan Horse	140
The Chinese Spy Balloon	141
Alibaba, Baidu, Huawei, TikTok, Tencent, Xiaomi, ZTE, and others	142
Theft of American Intellectual Property	145
Cybercriminals Weaponizing AI	145
Leaks of Classified Information	146
A History of Misreading the Tealeaves	149
AI and American Society	151
Conclusions / So What?	153
INDEX	156

> **Intelligence** is the ability to acquire and apply knowledge and skills.
>
> **Artificial Intelligence** is a branch of computer science dealing with the simulation of intelligent behavior in computers; or the capability of a machine to imitate intelligent human behavior
>
> **Merriam-Webster Dictionary**

> **Intelligence analysis:** a special or specific form of analysis normally carried out in a secret domain using special methodology and techniques to transform raw data into descriptions, explanations, and conclusions after considering multiple variables, for intelligence consumers, who normally are policy and decision makers in a nation/state.
>
> **Studies in Intelligence,**
> **Vol. 47, No. 3, 2003**

> AI is the most important tech advance in decades.
>
> **Bill Gates**
> **21 March 2023**
> **BBC**

> The information provided in this book was originally published in *open source*. The author did not use any classified or previously classified information. This book is heavily footnoted, and provides all the sources used to document findings.

Acknowledgements

During the writing of this book, I consulted specialists and people with other viewpoints to maintain objectivity. I am grateful for the moral support and encouragement provided by friends and colleagues. I am deeply appreciative of the assistance provided by Ambassador V. Manuel Rocha, who sent me numerous articles on a wide variety of subjects, in addition to his encouragement for my work in putting together this book. My cousin Joaquin M. Fermoselle assisted me to edit the manuscript. I thank my family and friends for their tolerance throughout the process of writing this book. Errors of fact and interpretation are strictly my own.

Executive Summary

Artificial Intelligence (AI), is the ability of machines to mimic the cognitive functions that humans and animals have for learning and using knowledge for problem-solving. Although the U.S. is assessed to be the leader in AI, nobody knows who the 'top dog' is, because a lot of the action is kept in secrecy. China and Russia are dedicating huge resources to achieve technological and military superiority. AI is data-centric. Whoever has the largest and most accurate database wins. It does not take very long to figure out that there is a new reality, and that traditional ethical and moral considerations are a thing of the past. Although the 'algorithmic warfare battlefield' is not yet here, it is not very far from becoming a reality. AI technology constitutes a significant transformative experience that impacts many areas for good and bad. But there is no confirmation of any instance in which robots killed anyone on their own without human involvement. Personal privacy has been lost, as financial institutions, credit card companies, banks, IT companies, airline and cruise companies, government agencies at all levels, and numerous other entities collect and share personal information. Social media is a warzone, now enhanced by AI. All kinds of nefarious actors use AI to trick people out of their money using very creative ways to create confusion. With the push of a button using AI, an organization or an individual can reach millions of people globally, and cause a crisis overnight. Sowing confusion using AI and social media platforms is a documented tactic of Russia and China. However, there has been considerable braggadocio, as some world leaders like to tout their accomplishments, but in reality, while some weaponized AI has been successful, others have underperformed. The FBI and the NCSC have released reports to raise awareness of how hostile actors use AI, fake profiles, and other forms of deception, to target people in government, business, and academia for recruitment and information gathering on a mass scale. AI is a present and increasingly future danger, but it is also a double edge sword. AI is a perfect tool for collecting intelligence on our enemies, as well as for counterintelligence, and it can be used to retaliate against wrongdoers. We are at the point in which nothing can be believed as real. It is unpredictable how emerging technologies will be used in the future. AI is not an antidote for a lack of common sense, sloppiness, carelessness, and poor judgment. Dysfunctional export controls of advanced technology and other failures to tighten security constitute a serious threat to the Free World and humanity. As if there was not enough to worry about, now there is speculation about scientists creating 'organoid intelligence' (OI) using real human brain cells!

Résumé

L'intelligence artificielle (IA) est la capacité des machines à imiter les fonctions cognitives que les humains et les animaux ont pour apprendre et utiliser les connaissances pour résoudre des problèmes. Bien que les États-Unis soient considérés comme le leader de l'IA, personne ne sait qui est le "Top Dog", car une grande partie de l'action est gardée secrète. La Chine et la Russie consacrent d'énormes ressources pour atteindre la supériorité technologique et militaire. L'IA est centrée sur les données. Celui qui a la plus grande base de données gagne. Il ne faut pas longtemps pour comprendre qu'il existe une nouvelle réalité et que les considérations éthiques et morales traditionnelles appartiennent au passé. Bien que le « champ de bataille de la guerre algorithmique » ne soit pas encore là, il n'est pas très loin de devenir une réalité. La technologie de l'IA constitue une expérience transformatrice importante qui a un impact positif et négatif sur de nombreux domaines. Mais il n'y a aucune confirmation d'un cas dans lequel des robots ont tué quelqu'un par eux-mêmes sans implication humaine. La vie privée a été perdue, car les institutions financières, les sociétés de cartes de crédit, les banques, les sociétés informatiques, les compagnies aériennes et de croisière, les agences gouvernementales à tous les niveaux et de nombreuses autres entités collectent et partagent des informations personnelles. Les médias sociaux sont une zone de guerre, désormais renforcée par l'IA. Toutes sortes d'acteurs néfastes utilisent l'IA pour tromper les gens avec leur argent en utilisant des moyens très créatifs pour créer la confusion. D'une simple pression sur un bouton utilisant l'IA, une organisation ou un individu peut atteindre des millions de personnes dans le monde et provoquer une crise du jour au lendemain. Semer la confusion en utilisant l'IA et les plateformes de médias sociaux est une tactique documentée de la Russie et de la Chine. Cependant, il y a eu beaucoup de fanfaronnade, car certains dirigeants mondiaux aiment vanter leurs réalisations, mais en réalité, alors que certaines IA militarisées ont réussi, d'autres ont sous-performé. Le FBI et le NCSC ont publié des rapports pour sensibiliser à la façon dont des acteurs hostiles utilisent l'IA, de faux profils et d'autres formes de tromperie, pour cibler des membres du gouvernement, des entreprises et des universités pour le recrutement et la collecte d'informations à grande échelle. L'IA est un danger présent et de plus en plus futur, mais c'est aussi une arme à double tranchant. L'IA est un outil parfait pour collecter des renseignements sur nos ennemis, ainsi que pour le contre-espionnage, et elle peut être utilisée pour exercer des représailles contre les malfaiteurs. Nous sommes au point où rien ne peut être cru comme réel. Il est imprévisible comment les technologies émergentes seront utilisées à l'avenir. L'IA n'est pas un antidote au manque de bon sens, à la négligence, à la négligence et au manque de jugement. Le dysfonctionnement des contrôles à l'exportation de la technologie de pointe et d'autres manquements au renforcement de la sécurité constituent une menace sérieuse pour le monde libre et l'humanité. Comme s'il n'y avait pas assez de raisons de s'inquiéter, il y a maintenant des spéculations sur les scientifiques créant une "intelligence organoïde" (OI) en utilisant de vraies cellules cérébrales humaines!

Resumen Ejecutivo

La Inteligencia Artificial (IA) es la capacidad de las máquinas para imitar las funciones cognitivas que tienen los humanos y los animales para aprender y usar el conocimiento para resolver problemas. Aunque se considera que EE. UU. es el líder en IA, nadie sabe quién es el "Top Dog", porque gran parte de la acción se mantiene en secreto. China y Rusia están dedicando enormes recursos para lograr la superioridad tecnológica y militar. La IA está centrada en los datos. Gana quien tenga la base de datos más grande. No lleva mucho tiempo darse cuenta de que hay una nueva realidad y que las consideraciones éticas y morales tradicionales son cosa del pasado. Aunque el 'campo de batalla de la guerra algorítmica' aún no está aquí, no está muy lejos de convertirse en una realidad. La tecnología de IA constituye una experiencia transformadora significativa que impacta muchas áreas para bien y para mal. Pero no hay confirmación de ningún caso en el que los robots hayan matado a alguien por su cuenta sin la participación humana. Se ha perdido la privacidad personal, ya que las instituciones financieras, las compañías de tarjetas de crédito, los bancos, las compañías de TI, las compañías aéreas y de cruceros, las agencias gubernamentales en todos los niveles y muchas otras entidades recopilan y comparten información personal. Las redes sociales son una zona de guerra, ahora mejorada por IA. Todo tipo de actores nefastos usan IA para engañar a las personas con su dinero usando formas muy creativas para crear confusión. Con solo presionar un botón usando IA, una organización o un individuo puede llegar a millones de personas en todo el mundo y causar una crisis de la noche a la mañana. Sembrar confusión usando IA y plataformas de redes sociales es una táctica documentada de Rusia y China. Sin embargo, ha habido una considerable jactancia, ya que a algunos líderes mundiales les gusta promocionar sus logros, pero en realidad, mientras que algunas IA armadas han tenido éxito, otras han tenido un desempeño inferior. El FBI y el NCSC han publicado informes para generar conciencia sobre cómo los actores hostiles utilizan la IA, los perfiles falsos y otras formas de engaño para apuntar a personas en el gobierno, las empresas y el mundo académico para el reclutamiento y la recopilación de información a gran escala. La IA es un peligro presente y cada vez más en el futuro, pero también es un arma de doble filo. La IA es una herramienta perfecta para recopilar inteligencia sobre nuestros enemigos, así como para la contrainteligencia, y puede usarse para tomar represalias contra los malhechores. Estamos en el punto en que nada se puede creer como real. Es impredecible cómo se utilizarán las tecnologías emergentes en el futuro. La IA no es un antídoto para la falta de sentido común, el descuido, y la falta de juicio. Los controles de exportación de tecnología avanzada son disfuncionales, que unidos a otras fallas constituyen una seria amenaza para el Mundo Libre y la humanidad. Como si no hubiera suficiente de qué preocuparse, ahora se especula que los científicos crean "inteligencia organoide" (OI) utilizando células cerebrales humanas reales.

Artificial Intelligence resembles a '*hydra*'

In Greek mythology, a '*hydra*' is a poisonous 9 headed snake, able to grow two more heads if one is cut off – the last of the heads is immortal...

Introduction

Artificial Intelligence (AI), is the ability of machines to mimic the cognitive functions that humans and animals have for learning and using knowledge for problem-solving. AI is considered the equivalent of the 4th Industrial Revolution.[1] No area of human activity is left untouched by it. AI can be weaponized for defensive, offensive, and criminal purposes. A weapon is anything that can be used to gain material, "mental," strategic, or tactical advantage over an adversary, including AI tools that can be used to double-cross human adversaries with deception. All areas of human activity are vulnerable. Some experts warn that as AI becomes more and more pervasive, it could affect the normal human decision-making process and impede people from thinking and making decisions in key aspects of their lives.[2]

AI weapons systems are purpose-built machines, software, or anything programmed for specific tasks, including tools in the arsenal of intelligence

---

[1] The first use of the term "*industrial revolution*," dates to 1840, and it was associated with a period of economic transformation through the introduction of power-driven machinery and innovations. It was used to describe the UK's economic development between 1760 and 1840. A second industrial revolution took place in the late 19th and early 20th centuries, with the introduction of new energy sources, the internal combustion engine, electricity, new metal alloys, plastics, and automated manufacturing. The 3rd industrial revolution began after the end of WWII, with the introduction of computers and digital systems, and rapid advances in communications, computing power, and other factors that led to the space age. The 4th industrial revolution is linked to the introduction of cyber-physical systems, and artificial intelligence.

[2] Jona Jaupi. Taking Over: AI machines could 'control humans' and make decisions for us if we don't act now, experts warn. *The U.S. Sun*. 24 December 2022.

designed to cause an individual to accept as true or valid what is false or invalid. AI weapon systems are a subset of information technology (IT), that can learn and apply knowledge in a similar way that humans and animals think, learn, and make decisions for self-defense or to attack an enemy. AI weapons, like any other segment of IT, are not immune to manipulation by malware, bugs, and hacking. AI-empowered weapons are in the hands of state actors, extremist organizations that use terrorism as a regular practice to achieve their goals, and all kinds of nefarious actors and criminals. AI weapons are operating with limited human intervention, and without ethics to decide whom to kill and whom not to. AI operates outside traditional values, ethics, and morals. Even wild animals are known to occasionally practice ethical behavior and compassion that resemble human emotions, but AI "machines" do not.[3]

> AI systems are susceptible to a range of disruptive and deceptive tactics that might be difficult to anticipate or quickly understand.
>
> **James Clapper,**
> Director of National Intelligence
> 9 February 2016

Reality has now outpaced science fiction with the advent of strategic and tactical autonomous weapons systems, also called *'killer robots,'* some driven by AI. As these weapons systems continue to advance, ethical and moral considerations about their use are increasing. Robotic weapons systems are increasing in variety and lethality, including so-called autonomous offensive and defensive weapons systems, some with limited human control.[4] Self-learning, self-targeting, and even self-replicating weapons systems are no longer science fiction. They exist and are emerging as a new *'existential'* danger to the international community.[5] But there is no confirmation of any instance in which robots killed anyone on their own without human involvement. The Creative and malicious use of AI is *'unpredictable.'* Factor into the equation speculation about scientists considering creating *'organic intelligence'* (OI) using real human brain cells.[6] [7]

---

[3] Tia Ghose. Animals Are Moral Creatures, Scientist Argues. *Livescience*. 15 November 2012 See also Mark Rowlands. Can Animals be Moral? Oxford University Press. 2012.

[4] Amitai Etzioni and Oren Etzioni. Pros and Cons of Autonomous Weapons Systems. Army University Press. Military Review. Pros and Cons of Autonomous Weapons Systems (army.mil)

[5] The *Merriam-Webster Dictionary* defines "*existential*" as *relating to, or affirming "existence." (The state or fact of having being especially independently of human consciousness and as contrasted with nonexistence.)* It is also defined as creating an identity and establishing meaningful relationships. searching for the meaning, purpose, and values of life... accepting anxiety as a condition of living, having the capacity for self-awareness, and as humans, having the capability to reflect and make choices.

[6] Hannah Docter-Loeb. Scientists Now Want to Create AU Using Real Human Brain Cells. *Vice.com*. 28 February 2023. Scientists Now Want to Create AI Using Real Human Brain Cells (vice.com)

[7] Roberto Molar Candanosa. Could future computers run on human brain cells? Johns Hopkins University. 28 February 2023. Could future computers run on human brain cells? | Hub (jhu.edu)

The best way to mitigate against the weaponization of AI is to be ahead of a diverse collection of rogue actors and develop countermeasures against a vast array of physical, cyber, and scientific threats. Weaponized AI systems, like any other weapons systems, aim to gain military superiority. The U.S. is the highest-ranked country in the knowledge and use of AI, followed by the UK, Finland, and Germany, but other countries, like China and Russia, are dedicating huge resources to achieve technological and military superiority using this vast field.[8] AI is creating a new algorithmic warfare battlefield that may or may not have human involvement and intervention.

Law enforcement, i.e., *"policing,"* is not transforming with the necessary speed to defeat criminal enterprises that have incorporated AI into their bag of tools and tricks. Cybercrime is increasing steadily and does not respect national borders, although the level of cybercrime activity can differ widely, and some countries, for example, Russia, have become important centers of criminal activity targeting victims all over the world. Due to the considerable underreporting of criminal activity by victims, it is challenging, if not impossible, to obtain a clear picture of the extent of the problem. Underreporting undermines the capacity of law enforcement entities to assess the extent of the problem and address the challenge appropriately. Without cooperation, it is very difficult to improve the effectiveness of counter-cybercrime programs, such as fraud, fake news, money laundering, and child pornography.

The Weaponization of AI is here to stay and is potentially inescapable. AI is advancing rapidly and is well on its way to changing all forms of warfare in the physical and cyber world. The use of AI in the conflict between Russia and Ukraine by both sides demonstrates the implications of technological advances that allow machines, i.e., computer-driven equipment to *"think"* and *"act"* on their own with minimal human interaction. In the arsenal of intelligence and counterintelligence operations, the *'art of deception and counter deception'* have been enhanced with the use of AI. Under the concept of *hybrid warfare*, AI-supported weapons systems can target military personnel, equipment, facilities, information systems, infrastructure, supply chains, and anything and everything critical and vulnerable *without ethical considerations*.

The future of warfare is dependent on speed based on weaponized AI – Making quick and accurate decisions based on a huge amount of data – and with weapons that can fire with a certain amount of autonomy from human interaction. China's Communist leaders are aggressively pursuing the goal of becoming the dominant power in the world in weaponized AI. Chinese leaders

---

[8] Russia was estimated to be investing about $14 million a year in AI weapons systems before the invasion of Ukraine in 2022, which seems to be a very low figure. After the invasion, and after repeated failures, the amount being invested has increased exponentially, but the amount has not been clearly assessed in open source. See: *CAN*. Artificial Intelligence and Autonomy in Russia. *CAN*. 8 September 2022. Special Edition; Samuel Bendett. Russia's Artificial Intelligence Boom May not Survive the War. Defense One. 15 April 2022.

have made AI a national strategic priority, as they position themselves to become dominant across the board. As Russian President Vladimir Putin clearly stated in 2017, "*Whoever reaches a breakthrough in developing artificial intelligence will come to dominate the world.*"

Weaponized AI has already been used to disseminate '*Deep Fake*' disinformation and generate fringe ideological discourse and cause multiple disruptions. Multiple forms of cyberattacks, including DDoS, ransomware, social engineering, hacking, spear phishing, whaling, and fake news distribution, are powered by weaponized AI. Mitigation of weaponized AI can only be achieved through the use of superior weaponized defensive AI systems. This project to describe what AI is all about has lasted three years, and demanded research on a scale that could not have been predicted. The very name '*artificial intelligence*' has become synonymous with the fear of the unknown.

TOP AI COMPANIES IN THE WORLD

Alphabet Inc. (U.S.)
Amazon Web Services, Inc. (U.S.)
Apple Inc. (U.S.)
Baidu, Inc. (China – PRC)
Cisco Systems Inc. (U.S.)
Facebook Inc. / Meta Platforms Inc. (U.S.)
General Electric (U.S.)
IBM (U.S.)
Intel (U.S.)
Micron Technology, Inc. (U.S.)
Microsoft Corporation (U.S.)
NVIDIA Corporation (U.S.)
Oracle Corporation (U.S.
Rockwell Automation Inc. (U.S.)
Samsun Group (South Korea)
SAP SE (Germany)
Siemens AG (Germany)

What is *Artificial Intelligence* (AI)?

Intelligence is defined as *'the natural ability of humans and animals to acquire and use knowledge and skills.'* Intelligence involves the *'cognitive functions'* or *'mental processes'* that allow humans and animals to obtain knowledge and information, store, process, transform, and use them to navigate the world. A key component of intelligence is the *'ability to maintain alertness to certain aspects of the environment,'* to correctly recognize and attribute meaning to previously learned information through the combined use of senses, including visual recognition, sounds, touch, smell, and taste. Intelligence fuels the *decision-making process,* based on the assumptions, perceptions, preferences, morals, and values of the decision-maker.

> Whoever reaches a breakthrough in developing artificial intelligence will come to dominate the world.
>
> Vladimir Putin
> 1 Sept. 2017

Artificial Intelligence (AI) is the ability of machines to mimic or simulate the cognitive functions that humans and animals have for learning and using knowledge for problem-solving. AI combines the use of machines, i.e., computers, with databases to perform tasks, normally carried out by humans, including speech recognition, biometrics and visual perception, language translation, and other functions across many fields. The Merriam-Webster Dictionary defines AI as "a branch of computer science dealing with the simulation of intelligent behavior in computers," or "the capability of a machine to imitate intelligent human behavior." However, machines do not have a working set of morals and values to drive the decision-making process.

AI is constantly *'morphing'* into more advanced forms. At some point in the not-so-distant future, self-driving cars, or *"autonomous vehicles,"* may be possible. Several companies have already produced advanced prototypes, including Tesla, GM, Ford, and Mercedes-Benz, and companies like Google have been investing in the concept starting as far back as 1995. *Google Translate* has become an excellent tool to translate from one language to another, and progress continues to be made to the point that in the future human translators/interpreters may be replaced by more accurate machines. Several companies, including Google, Microsoft, and Amazon have made huge advances in voice recognition with such products as *Assistant, Cortana,* and *Alexa.* Robots' hand dexterity has continued to advance, with an increasing ability to mimic human hands. Video facial images can now be tinkered with to create high-fidelity realistic human expressions. Humans are already finding themselves working alongside machines. Rogue actors with nefarious intentions can already defeat advanced security systems designed to protect network traffic. [9] [10] [11]

Intelligent Automation (IA)

Intelligent automation (IA) is the *'automation of business processes,'* through a combination of AI and *'robotic process automation'* (RPA). Repetitive tasks are broken down, to be addressed by robots logically, to replace humans in manufacturing and many types of business processes. IBM defines IA as the *"use of automation technologies – artificial intelligence (AI), business process management (BPM), and robotic process automation (RPA) – to streamline and scale decision-making across organizations."*[12] [13] [14] [15]

IA is the combination of AI and automation to transform repetitive tasks normally carried out by humans into processes that can be carried out by robots. It involves the transformation of human actions into digital actions through the collaborative convergence of technologies. IA is driven by a shortage of workers willing to accept employment that involves repetitive tasks and low wages. It is also driven by the goal of companies to reduce costs and increase their profit margins. Although IA has been around for many years, and its use is accelerating, it continues to suffer from the shortage of qualified experts in the technology.

Many companies are using IA for multiple tasks, including accelerating automation, accounting and financial management, answering common questions, automating repetitive tasks, classification of documents, customer services, data extraction, extract information from electronic forms, extract data from online forms, identifying inefficiencies, invoice reminders, make data-driven decisions, monitoring web and social media traffic, natural language processing, pattern recognition, predictive analytics, pricing models, process documents,

---

[9] James O'Malley. The 10 most important breakthroughs in Artificial Intelligence. *Techradar.* 10 January 2018.

[10] Rohit Yadav. Top 7 Artificial Intelligence Breakthroughs We Saw in 2019. Top 7 Artificial Intelligence Breakthroughs We Saw In 2019 (analyticsindiamag.com)

[11] Bernard Marr. The 7 Biggest Artificial Intelligence (AI) Trends in 2022. *Forbes.* 20 September 2021.

[12] IBM. What is intelligence automation? What is Intelligent Automation? | IBM

[13] David Schatsky. Intelligent automation: A new era of innovation. *Deloitte.* 23 January 2014. Intelligent automation: A new era of innovation | Deloitte Insights

[14] Innodata. What Does Intelligent Automation Really Mean? Innodata. (1) New Messages! (innodata.com)

[15] Damien Webb. Jargon buster: What does intelligent automation really mean? Ricoh. Jargon buster: what does intelligent automation really mean? (ricoh.co.uk)

process mining, validate information from emails, and voice-activated customer service over phone lines, among many other tasks.

Definition of Data

Data is defined as *pieces of information, facts, quantities, characters, symbols, names, and figures,* and since the start of the computer age, *circa 1946,* the term is used to mean *"transmissible and storable computer information."* Data is the plural for *datum*, a Latin word meaning *"something given."* In Spanish, the term *"datos"* is used. In French, the term used is *"données."* In Italian, the word for data is *"dati."* In German, the word for data is *"daten,"* in Russian, data is *"данных,"* and in Chinese 数 据 (*shù jù*). In other words, data is a collection of information, including facts, numbers, and images, visualized or analyzed using tools, such as a computer.

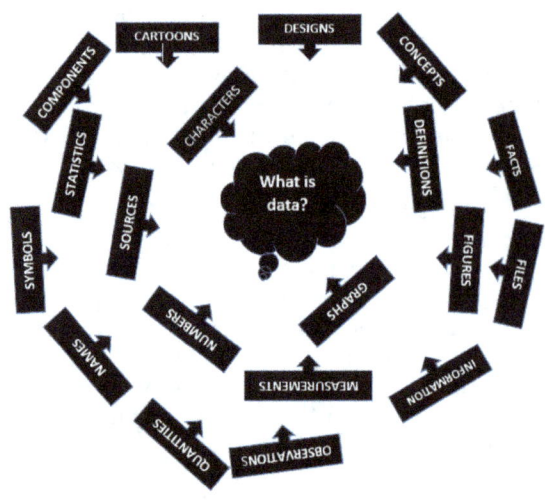

Data is collected for multiple purposes, stored and transmitted in the form of electrical signals, and recorded in multiple0 forms of recording media. *Data integration* is the process of extracting and combining data from multiple disparate sources into a single, unified view for analysis. The analysis of collected data has revolutionized the way humans use it for multiple purposes, including ethical considerations for its use. Machines analyze available data based on how they have been programmed to consider the facts on hand, without ethical ramifications involved in the process.

Data Validation, Metrics, and Big Data

Data validation refers to a *process of confirming, affirming, corroborating, or documenting the quality of the data.'* The concept surfaced at the U.S. Department of Defense (DOD) during his tenure as Secretary of Defense of Robert McNamara (1963-1968). He hired a group of bright young men, often referred to as the *'Whiz Kids,'* to help him improve the management of DOD, particularly in operations research, computing, and associated technologies. They are credited with the 'invention' of the concept of '*Big Data.*' [16] He had a passion for numbers and their meaning. He was particularly interested in maximizing the effectiveness of air operations, as he had served in WWII in the Air Force, and reached the rank of captain. In the age of AI, the efforts of Secretary McNamara to validate data is more important than ever. Big Data can be more fallible than people expect and has to be tamed by the human hands of a hyper-rational manager. But how can that be done in the world of AI, when machines are expected to act on their own without human interaction? [17] [18]

To explain what Secretary McNamara had in mind, let's use the example of any car of any brand. When a person purchases a new car, it is just like any other car that came out of the production line. However, every car owner drives, acts, and behaves in a particular way. After driving the vehicle for about three years, the rubber on the accelerator and the brake pedals will show a peculiar way of showing use. The rubber will be worn out in a very peculiar way, and so will other car parts. The weight and the way of seating of the driver will wear the driver's seat peculiarly. Car systems, such as the brakes, will also show wear and tear based on the driving style of the owner. If one compares equal cars of the same brand and style that came out of the same factory one after the other and looked alike, after three to five years, they will no longer look alike. The vehicles will show considerable differences in wear and tear based on who drove them.

Secretary McNamara suspected that when a pilot is assigned a particular fighter plane, for example, a similar process takes place, in which the plane starts to show certain wear and tear and performance directly related to the way the pilot behaved. Secretary McNamara wanted to validate the statistical data, to see how it reflected the habits of the pilot. He had a data-driven approach and surrounded himself with the group of Whiz Kids, which could assist him in finding ways to improve operations. This was all related to financial planning and improvements in management, and shaping a modern defense strategy with improved economic analysis, operations research, computing, and game theory. The Whiz Kids worked as DOD contractors, employed by the RAND Corporation.

---

[16] Tristan Gaston-Breton. How Robert McNamara and the Whiz Kids Invented Big Data. *Worldcrunch.com*. 13 September 2016. How Robert McNamara And The Whiz Kids Invented Big Data – Worldcrunch

[17] Kenneth Cukier & Victor Mayer-Schonberger. The Dictatorship of Data: Robert McNamara epitomizes the hyper-rational executive led astray by numbers. *MIT*. 31 May 2013. The Dictatorship of Data | MIT Technology Review

[18] Jonatan Salem Baskin. According to U.S. Big Data, We Won the Vietnam War. *Forbes*. 25 July 2014. According To U.S. Big Data, We Won The Vietnam War (forbes.com)

Weaponizing 'Big Data' with AI

According to the *Merriam-Webster Dictionary*, "*Big Data*" is defined as *an accumulation of data that is too large and complex for processing by traditional database management tools.* In other words, the term means a large accumulation of complex data, which makes it very difficult to analyze and visualize due to the volume, variety, and velocity in which it is acquired. One of the challenges of '*big data*' is the challenge to evaluate its quality. Size does not necessarily mean that it is accurate. The world is now dealing with "*zettabytes*" of data, defined as: a unit of digital information storage used to denote the size of data, equivalent to 1,024 exabytes or 1,000,000.000,000,000,000,000 bytes. By 2025, global data creation is projected to grow to more than 180 zettabytes.[19]

AI could be the solution to transform a huge amount of complex data into '*actionable insight*s' and gain a real advantage. A huge amount of collected data goes to waste because it is never used. An AI '*engine*' could be fed data, to be sorted with a reduced need for human intervention. Big Data and AI could significantly complement each other, and reduce the uselessness of data that does not get analyzed because there is no viable human way to do it. Humans cannot efficiently make use of Big Data.[20] AI and related machine learning systems are dependent on Big Data to function. AI is a data hog.[21] AI is irrelevant without Big Data.

AI can detect anomalies, recognize patterns, and predict future outcomes using laws of probability.[22] For example, computers can process recordings in multiple languages, translate them, and assist in helping to analyze huge amounts of human language data. AI can also process huge amounts of health information, for example during a pandemic, to track how a virus is spreading, and use predictive modeling to determine if it is the result of a natural occurrence or a weaponized virus. However, AI depends on the availability of '*Big Data.*'

---

[19] Petroc Taylor. *Statista.* 8 September 2022. Total data volume worldwide 2010-2025 | Statista

[20] Alex Melnichuk. How Big Data and AI Work Together. NCUBE.Com. 21 January 2020. https://ncube.com/blog/big-data-and-ai

[21] Nick Ismail. The success of artificial intelligence depends on data. *Information Age.* 28 April 2018. The success of artificial intelligence depends on data. (information-age.com)

[22] Analytics Insight. Using Artificial Intelligence in Big Data. Analyticsinsight.com. 3 June 2020. https://www.analyticsinsight.net/using-artificial-intelligence-in-big-data/

What are Systems?

Systems are a set of *'things,'* interrelated elements, or *'principles'* interacting or working together to achieve something. The *Merriam-Webster Dictionary* defines *'systems,'* as a *set of things working together as parts of a mechanism or an interconnecting network.'* There are multiple types of systems. For example, economic, information, political, and social systems. Systems represent an organization of procedures and resources that accomplish a set of specific functions. It has also been defined as a set of principles and procedures, methodology, and techniques to do something.

In information technology (IT), a system includes hardware, software, data, applications (apps), communications, and technical personnel. A *'computer system,'* includes multiple components, including headphones, keyboards, microchips, monitors, motherboards, operating systems, plotters, printers, projectors, software, sound cards, speakers, video cards, and other components. So, what is the meaning of all of these definitions of *'systems*? A system is something designed or organized to achieve a common purpose. Artificial Intelligence *'systems'* are systems designed to carry out human-like tasks, without the need for a human to intervene.

Systems Theory

'Systems theory' is the interdisciplinary study of systems. Every system is formed by interdependent components, which can be natural or human-made, and is defined by its purpose, function, and role, as well as how it interacts with other systems. System theory is based on the interacting processes of internal components and how they interact or influence other systems. Systems interact with other systems....and influence and interact with them. The concept of *'system theory'* is useful to study life...in a very complex world, and is used to study and explain very complex phenomena, formed by many interconnected interdisciplinary systems.[23]

System of Systems (SoS)

'System of systems' is defined as *a collection of complex task-oriented systems.'* The concept brings together several systems to accomplish a purpose that component systems cannot accomplish independently. The *Merriam-Webster Dictionary* defines SoS as *'a regularly interacting or independent groups of items forming a unified whole.'* It goes on to explain SoS as a *group of devices or artificial objects or an organization forming a network especially for distributing*

---

[23] Ludwig von Bertalanffy. *General System Theory*. New York: Barnes & Noble. 1968.

something or serving a common purpose,' such as a *telephone system*, a *heating system*, a *highway system*, or a *computer system*.

Another way to explain SoS is as a collection of independent systems, part of a larger system, that has unique capabilities to deliver a solution or product in collaboration with one another. A collection of independent systems works together as part of a more complex system of systems to accomplish a given task. SoS requires 'systems thinking' that allows for joint work of several systems to accomplish a specific task. SoS applications are used widely, for example, by government agencies, such as the Department of Defense, NASA, the Department of Transportation, and the Federal Aviation Administration. SoS is also widely used in the private sector, for example, in banking and finance, the news media, and in healthcare. AI is used to empower an SoS to accomplish tasks without the need for human intervention.

After the terrorist attacks of 9/11/2001, this author became a Systems of Systems Analyst (SOSA) at the U.S. Joint Forces Command (USJFCOM) and participated in the training and deployment of the concept of *'Effects-Based Approach to Operations* (EBAO) to all the regional combatant commands.[24] *Standing Joint Forces Headquarters* were set up at all the regional commands, after prior training by the first team that was set up at USJFCOM.[25]

Normally, a systems analyst, is responsible for determining the computing needs of a client, and translating them into system specifications. However, that was not the case with EBAO. It involved the concept of military operations conceived and planned in a *system of systems* framework, taking into account a full range of direct and indirect effects, achieved through the application of military, diplomatic, economic, information, and psychological instruments. Contrary to conventional military doctrine and approaches to the use of force to annihilate an enemy, the EBAO doctrine was to aim at achieving a desired strategic objective (effect) by manipulating the political, economic, social, and information systems- using a *systemic approach* by focusing on key centers of gravity. The goal was to change the nature of warfare.

However, during a time of war, it was not a good time to be experimenting with and deploying a new concept of warfare. The U.S. and its allies were at war in Afghanistan and Iraq against Muslim extremist organizations that used terrorism as a preferred and frequent weapon of war. These concepts predate progress in AI technology, and by 2008, the EBAO concept was taken out of military doctrine, and it was determined that EBO was fundamentally flawed, in

---

[24] USJFCOM was created in 1993 and closed in 2011. The command was created to focus on the transformation of U.S. military capabilities. NOTE: EBAO was defined as an *'a process for obtaining a desired strategic outcome or effect on the enemy through the synergistic and cumulative application of the full range of military and nonmilitary capabilities at all levels of conflict.'*

[25] U.S. Central Command, U.S. European Command, U.S. Northern Command, U.S. Indo-Pacific Command, U.S. Southern Command, U.S. Special Operations Command, U.S. Strategic Command, and U.S. Transportation Command.

part, because there were too many interpretations and it created a lot of confusion.[26] The analytical tools and instruments to affect the behavior of an enemy beyond old-fashion military force were not available. The systems-of-systems analysis basic to the Operational Net Assessment, and EBO became somewhat of a distraction, and problematic when working in a multinational war effort.[27]

System validation

The term '*system*' has been improperly used and ill-defined for a very long time. '*System validation*,' has also been ill-defined, misunderstood, and misused. The best way to explain these concepts is by providing some examples. On 4 August 1977, President Jimmy Carter signed into law the creation of the U.S. Department of Energy (DOE). The U.S. Congress wanted to bring together over 30 separate energy-related functions that had been spread over various government agencies. One of the agencies created under DOE was the Energy Information Administration (EIA). The purpose of EIA was to collect and analyze energy data and forecast future energy needs, inventories, demand and supply, and assessments of price.

The genesis of both, DOE and EIA, were the oil market disruptions in 1974, which resulted from the Arab-Israeli war of 1973. Congress wanted to have the most accurate estimates of energy-related data. Before the creation of DOE and EIA, other agencies, such as the Bureau of Mines, housed under the Department of the Interior, generated important energy data, but mainly by gathering data from multiple sources, sometimes in *ad hoc* impromptu, or improvised ways which affected the quality of the data.

For example, for state governments, oil and gas production are revenue basing categories. Crude oil and natural gas were produced in about ten states, which taxed the production, and as a result, the data was fairly accurate. States like Texas, Louisiana, North Dakota, New Mexico, California, and Alaska, where over 90 percent of production was achieved, had very accurate data, because as an important revenue category data quality was important. However, for other states with much lower energy production, such as West Virginia and Pennsylvania, production data were gathered on an *ad hoc* basis, and the data quality was limited. Congress wanted EIA to 'validate' key information systems, such as oil and gas production, oil imports, refinery runs, and the burning of

---

[26] General James N. Mattis. "USJFCOM Commander's Guidance for Effects-Based Operations. Parameters 38, no. 3 (2008), doi:10.55540/0031-1723.2437. Note: General Mattis, now retired, was the Commander of the U.S. Central Command, responsible for military operations in the Middle East, North Africa, and Central Asia. He did not like the EBO concept and canned it. In 2016, he was appointed by President Donald Trump as Secretary of Defense. He resigned effective 28 February 2019.

[27] The Office of Net Assessment (ONA) was founded in 1973, with the task of providing long-term comparative assessments of trends, key competitions, risks, opportunities, and the future of military capabilities.

fuel by major energy consumers, such as power plants. At best, the data before 1977, was no more than about 98 percent accurate.

This author was hired as a contractor in 1978, to work on a project to determine the accuracy of these information systems. It did not take very long to find out that there was no such thing as a *"crude oil production information system."* The term 'system' implies that there was a need, and a process or system was formally designed to collect the most accurate data. Instead, a very *ad hoc* system was used by the Bureau of Mines. Data from the top-producing states was very accurate, but not perfect. One of the first things done was to travel to Oklahoma City, to meet with the Interstate Oil & Gas Compact Commission, composed of governors of oil and gas-producing states. During the visit, all kinds of unexpected issues were discussed.

For example, native American tribes, are independent nations, within the United States. They do not pay taxes to the states or the Federal Government. For example, the Osage Nation, located in northeastern Oklahoma, is one of about a dozen Native American tribal nations that have significant oil and gas reserves and production. If they do not pay taxes on production to the state government, do they have to report their production statistics to anybody? Did the native energy-producing tribes work out different agreements or 'systems' to turn over their energy production data? How did that affect the quality of national oil and gas production statistics?

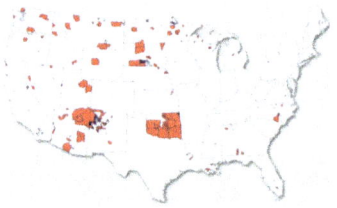

Native American Independent Nations

How could EIA, and DOE have accurate and validated production statistics, if there were potentially serious gaps in reporting? What the Bureau of Mines managed before 1977, was not a true *'information system'* with validated statistics. Why? Because before the energy crisis in 1974, the issue was not a priority. What was the outcome? Is domestic energy production data in 2023 any better or more accurate than in 1977?

What are computers?

Computers are 'electronic programmable devices that manipulate information, and can store and process data at high speed, based on prescribed mathematical operations, typically in a binary form.' Since WWII, computers have transformed from large mega boxes to desktops, laptops, smart cell phones, and miniature chips. From the start when governments, the military, and academic institutions were the prime drivers in the advancement of computer science, the field has grown to a broad range of technology fields. Right from the start, computers, and weapons systems have been linked, and science fiction books and movies have speculated on what may happen on the battlefield of the future.

The Abacus
The history of early computing goes back over 4,000 years to China, where a wooden rack with metal rods with beads was invented to make arithmetic calculations. The first modern computer was the Mark I, manufactured in 1944 during WWII by IBM and Harvard University.

Computers have revolutionized the way humans get information (data) and interact with one another. Data is not necessarily *'factual information,'* even if used for reasoning, discussion, calculation, or to help in decision-making, or information in an electronic form.[28] There are multiple forms of data, including personal or individual data, behavioral data, attitudinal data, and engagement data. It is estimated that, by 2024, the total volume of data created and consumed worldwide will reach 149 zettabytes.[29] (A *'zettabyte'* is a multiple of the unit byte that measures digital storage, and it is equivalent to 1,000,000,000,000,000,000,000 [10^{21}] bytes.[30] The integrity of any analysis based on data depends on the accuracy of the information. Any credible answers resulting from any type of analysis depend on the quality of the data used. AI depends on the availability and quality of data. Since WWII, when the *Electronic Numerical Integrator and Computer* (ENIAC), the first known electronic general-purpose computer, they have become increasingly powerful, faster, and smaller.[31] The dynamic forces that emerged during, and after WWII, led to the

---

[28] *Cambridge Dictionary.* https://dictionary.cambridge.org/us/dictionary/english/number

[29] Nemanja Jovancic. 5 Data Collection Methods for Obtaining Quantitative and Qualitative Data. Leadquizzes.com. 10 May 2021. https://www.leadquizzes.com/blog/data-collection-methods/

[30] Max Freedman. How businesses are collecting data (And what they're doing with it). *Businessnewsdaily.com.* 17 June 2020.

[31] The ENIAC inventors were John W. Mauchly and J. Presper Eckert.

so-called 'birth' of AI around 1950.[32] [33] [34] The pioneers in AI were Alan Mathison Turing (1912-1954), a British logician and mathematician, and American logician and mathematician Alonzo Church (1903-1995). They are credited with contributing to the advancements of mathematical logic and computer science, and the birth of AI. The so-called Church-Turing thesis stated that *'everything humanly computable can also be computed by a machine.'*

The first laptop came about in 1981, introduced into the market by Adam Osborne and EPSON. Increasingly powerful, high-performance, and more portable computers continue to be introduced to address specific challenges. The computer revolution is an ongoing process and involves machine learning and quantum computing. As computers continue to become ever more powerful, so thus AI capabilities, including predictive and preventative analytics.

---

[32] Alok Aggarwal, Alan Turing, Herbert A. Simon, Marvin Minsky. The Birth of AI and The First AI Hype Cycle. *KDnuggets*. 14 February 2018. The Birth of AI and The First AI Hype Cycle - KDnuggets

[33] Sintia Radu. Despite Chinese Efforts, the U.S. Still Leads in AI. *U.S. News & World Report*. 19 August 2019. Executive Order on Maintaining American Leadership in Artificial Intelligence – The White House (archives.gov)

[34] Naomi Davies. Index shows US is winning the AI race – but for how long? *Investment Monitor*. 10 November 2021. Index shows US still leading world for AI - Investment Monitor

CONTRIBUTORS TO THE CREATION OF ARTIFICIAL INTELLIGENCE

Blaise Pascal
1623-1662

Gottfried Wilhelm Von Leibniz
1646-1716

Charles Babbage
1791-1871

Ada Lovelace
1815-1852

Herman Hollerith
1860-1929

Warren S. McCulloch
1898-1969

Walter Pitts
1923-1969

Over the centuries, different devices came about to make calculations. The *Pascaline* was invented in 1642 by French mathematician and philosopher Blaise Pascal. It consisted in a wooden box with gears and wheels to make mathematical calculation. In 1673, Gottfried Wilhelm Leibniz, a German mathematician and philosopher introduced an improvement on the Pascaline, which was renamed the *Leibniz wheel*. It replaced the original based on gears with fluted drums. In 1820, Charles Babbage created the so-called *Difference Engine*, a steam-powered calculating machine used to solve numerical and logarithmic tables. Babbage later created the *Analytical Engine* in 1830, that took input from punch cards, and was able to solve mathematical problems and store data in an indefinite memory. The English mathematician and writer Augusta Ada King (Countess of Lovelace), worked with Babbage and is credited with first recognizing the potential for the Analytical Engine to perform an algorithm, namely, a sequence of rigorous instructions, to solve specific problem or perform a computation. In 1890, Herman Hollerith, an American statistician, invented a *Tabulating Machine*, also using punch cards, to compute statistics and record data. Hollerith invention eventually led to the creation of IBM in 1924. In 1930, the *Differential Analyzer*, a machine that used vacuum tubes which switched electrical impulses to do calculations, was introduced by Vannevar Bush. By the start of WWII in 1939, the race was on to invent machines that could make massive calculations using huge amounts of data. American mathematician and logician Walter Pitts published a treatise on neural networks and automatons, indicating that each neuron in the brain is a simple digital processor and the brain as a whole performs as a computing machine.

What is Quantum Computing?

A *'quantum computer'* is a computer that is based on *'quantum mechanics,'* to solve complex problems and process algorithms much faster and beyond the capacity of regular or classical computers to solve. They make use of subatomic particles to store and process information. According to the *Merriam-Webster Dictionary*, quantum computers take advantage of the quantum properties of *'qubits'* to perform certain types of calculations extremely quickly compared to conventional computers.[35] Another way of explaining these types of computers is that they make use of the quantum states of electrons and other subatomic particles to store and process information as *'quantum bits,'* and have the capacity to perform many different computations simultaneously. While normal or traditional computers carry out or 'compute' operations for each state separately, they can carry multiple operations in superposition and all at once. They leverage the laws of *'quantum mechanics,'* and assist in such difficult things as breaking so-called *'unbreakable codes.'*

Quantum computers process information in microseconds working in absolute zero temperature. They are *'unhackable,'* and can solve complex mathematical problems, including all forms of encryption, making them useless. They can defeat at quantum speed classical computer algorithms, using *'qubit'* as the basic unit of information, instead of 'bits' used by traditional binary systems. They represent a new frontier in computing, but there is a shortage of experts qualified to exploit this technology.

To understand how these computers work, one would have to understand the principles of quantum mechanics, and such things as the energy levels of atoms and subatomic particles called *'quanta.'*[36] Using the principles of quantum mechanics these computers can do simultaneous calculations extremely fast. They represent the key to being the global *top dog* by providing the key to breaking through cryptography and finding the defense-related secrets of competing military powers and intelligence organizations. Harnessing this technology, mixed with artificial intelligence algorithms, is the key to global supremacy through cracking the outmost secrets of competing world powers. However, as of 2023, most things tied to quantum computing are experimental. Enhanced computation using subatomic particles to store and process

---

[35] Quantum computer Definition & Meaning - Merriam-Webster

[36] *Quanta* is the plural of *quantum*. It is defined as a discrete quantity of energy, proportional in magnitude to the frequency of the radiation it represents. Britannica defines quantum in physics, *as a discrete natural unit, or packet of energy, charge, angular momentum, or other physical property.* Quantum | Definition & Facts | Britannica

information is still a bridge too far, but top scientists are closing in, but conceptualizing the technology is challenging.

To illustrate the importance of quantum computing, on 4 May 2022, a *National Security Memorandum on Promoting United States Leadership in Quantum Computing While Mitigating Risks to Vulnerable Cryptographic Systems* was issued by President Biden, to advance quantum technologies. The main purpose was to direct all branches of the Federal Government to take specific actions to protect the process of migrating vulnerable computer systems to quantum-resistant cryptography. It points out the need to maintain a competitive advantage in quantum computing and QIS.[37]

What are Computer Chips?

Semiconductors or '*computer chips*' are the basic building block for AI. The mastery of the semiconductor sector is the key to AI. The future of intelligent machines depends on advances in this technology. The ability of semiconductors to run, test, process, and store data is basic to AI. For that reason, all world powers focus on the semiconductor sector. They are critical to the economy and for the national security of the United States.[38]

A typical computer chip is an '*electronic device*' of less than one square inch, usually made of a wafer of silicon or some other semiconducting material, on which an '*integrated circuit*' is embedded or engraved.[39] [40]They are referred to as *chips*, *microchips*, microprocessors, *silicon chips*, and *integrated circuits* (IC). They have been around since about 1961. Chips contain *transistors* or *electronic switches* and other components made of semiconductor materials, normally silicon, that have very fast decision-making capabilities. There are many types of computer chips produced at present time with different capabilities. They are the '*brains*' inside many things, from household appliances to vehicles, medical

---

[37] The White House. President Joe Biden. *National Security Memorandum on Promoting United States Leadership in Quantum Computing While Mitigating Risks to Vulnerable Cryptographic Systems*. 4 May 2022. National Security Memorandum on Promoting United States Leadership in Quantum Computing While Mitigating Risks to Vulnerable Cryptographic Systems | The White House

[38] U.S. Senate Republican Policy Committee. Semiconductors: Key to Economic and National Security. Senate RPC. 29 April 2021. Semiconductors: Key to Economic and National Security (senate.gov)

[39] According to the *Merriam-Webster Dictionary*, an integrated circuit is *a tiny complex of electronic components and their connections that is produced in or on a small slice of material (such as silicon)*. Integrated circuit Definition & Meaning - Merriam-Webster

[40] *Silicon* is a '*chemical element*' with the 'atomic number 14. A total of 118 chemical elements have been identified as of 2023. Elements cannot be broken down into simpler substances. Silicon is a nonmetal with semiconducting properties, used for making electronic circuits, or computer chips.

devices, cell telephones, weapons, and yes... computers.[41] [42] Following the start of the COVID pandemic in early 2020, global supply chain disruptions surfaced, which included computer chip shortages, causing many factories to shut down production, including vehicle manufacturers and consumer electronics companies.[43] To complicate matters more, with the start of the Russian invasion of Ukraine in February 2022, Ukraine's exports of neon gas, which is used by lasers used in chip-making were disrupted.[44] However, by January 2023, a glut of computer chips was developing in global markets.

The top manufacturer of chips in the world is the **Taiwan Semiconductor Manufacturing Company** (TSMC), founded in 1987. It manufactures about 54 percent of the chips made in the world and is the principal supplier to leading technology companies. **Samsung Electronics** is the second largest manufacturer of chips, with about a 17 percent global market share. In 2022, the company introduced the production of an advanced 3-nanometer process node applying so-called *Gate-All-Around* (GAA) transistor architecture, enhancing chip performance.[45] Samsung's chip production is based in Seoul, South Korea. The third largest manufacturer of computer chips is **Global Foundries**, with about 7 percent market share, headquartered in New York. It manufactures in the U.S., Singapore, Burlington, Malta, and Germany. The company was the result of AMD spinning off its chip manufacturing in 2008. IBM sold its microelectronics business to Global Foundries in 2014. The principal investor in the company is the Abu Dhabi sovereign wealth fund Mubadala Investment Co.[46] Ranked fourth in chip manufacturing is **Intel**. The company was founded in 1968 and is headquartered in Santa, Clara, California. Intel produced the first microprocessor chips for commercial purposes in 1971.

---

[41] Govind Bhutada. The Top 10 Semiconductor Companies by Market Share. Visualcapitalist.com 14 December 2021. The Top 10 Semiconductor Companies by Market Share (visualcapitalist.com)

[42] Thomas Alsop. Leading semiconductor foundries revenue share worldwide 2019-2022, by quarter. Statista. 1 July 2022. Top semiconductor foundries market share 2022 | Statista

[43] Katie Canales. Here's why there's a global computer chip shortage that is slamming automakers during the pandemic. Businessinsider.com. 6 February 2021. Why Is There a Computer Chip Shortage? Cars, Tech Face Supply-Chain Issues (businessinsider.com)

[44] Chris Isidore. Why the global supply chain mess is getting so much worse. CNN. 30 March 2022. Why the global supply chain mess is getting so much worse | CNN Business

[45] Samsung Begins Chip Production Using 3nm Process Technology with GAA Architecture. 30 June 2022. Samsung Begins Chip Production Using 3nm Process Technology with GAA Architecture – Samsung Global Newsroom

[46] Stephen Nellis and Krystal Hu. Chipmaker GlobalFoundries valued at $26 b in lackluster Nasdaq debut. *Reuters*. 28 October 2021. Chipmaker GlobalFoundries valued at $26 bln in lackluster Nasdaq debut | Reuters

It specializes in producing chips that are found in most personal computers, including Acer, Dell, HP, and Lenovo.[47]

The fifth largest manufacturer of semiconductor chips is **Qualcomm**, an American company founded in 1985, and headquartered in San Diego, California. The company is a key player in wireless communications, and its chips are used by many cell telephone manufacturers. Qualcomm chips are used in laptops, smartphones, vehicles, watches, and other technology products. The company has been selling into the Chinese market for at least 20 years and has been at the center of international disputes between the U.S. and the PRC related to intellectual property. Qualcomm has been involved in multiple litigations with other IT companies and government oversight institutions over patent and intellectual property rights for many years, including the U.S. Federal Trade Commission (FTC).[48]

Other significant global manufacturers of computer chips are *Micron, Broadcom, Nvidia*, and *Texas Instruments*. Despite the serious global shortage of computer chips that developed with the COVID pandemic in 2020 and the start of the Russian invasion of Ukraine, by December 2022, the shortages came to an end, linked to a slump in demand. Micron, the largest American manufacturer of memory chips was faced with a market glut that replaced the shortages of 2020 to early 2022.[49] The market glut was the result of chip manufacturing stepping up production to meet demand, inflation, and the start of a global economic downturn. The enactment of the so-called *'CHIPS and Science Act'* in the U.S. in August 2022, was in part the cause of the market glut. Members of Congress wanted to revitalize and boost chip production in the U.S.[50] The legislation was aimed at producing in the U.S. chips to reduce the reliance on approximately 75 percent on imports, mostly from Asia.

Broadcom is another American company that manufactures a wide range of computer chips. It is headquartered in San Jose, California. Broadcom has a history of conflicts with both, the EU, the UK, the FTC, and the U.S. Securities and Exchange Commission (SEC), due to allegations of a tendency to try to restrict competition and monopolize markets. Originally, it was a division of

---

[47] Heather Hall. The 10 largest Chip Manufacturers in the World and What They Do. *History-Computer.com*. 30 November 2022. The 10 Largest Chip Manufacturers in the World and What They Do - History-Computer

[48] Ikenna Emewu. Qualcomm, largest chip maker aims at higher profits. *Africachinapresscentre.org*. 6 November 2021. Qualcomm, largest chip maker aims at higher profits | AFRICA CHINA ECONOMY (africachinapresscentre.org)

[49] Ian King. Micron to cut 10% of workforce as demand for computer chips slumps, *Yahoo!Finance*. 21 December 2022. Micron to Cut 10% of Workforce as Demand for Computer Chips Slumps (yahoo.com)

[50] CNBC. Micron to invest $40 billion in U.S. chip manufacturing. CNBC. 9 August 2022. Micron to invest $40 billion in U.S. chip manufacturing (cnbc.com)

Hewlett-Packard. The company has triggered national security concerns by U.S. authorities for alleged ties with the PRC and the Chinese chipmaker Huawei. Broadcom produces a wide range of products for alternative energy systems, DDR memory interfaces, mainframe computer operations, displays, hard disk controllers, telecommunications, and Wi-Fi/Bluetooth/GPS devices. As of 2021, Broadcom was estimated to have a 3.2 share of the global semiconductor market.[51]

Texas Instruments, an American company based in Dallas, is one of the top global manufacturers of computer chips, particularly analog chips and embedded processors, as well as some consumer electronics, particularly handheld calculators, software, and AI. As of 2021, it was estimated that the company had a global market share of 2.9 percent of the semiconductor market.[52]

---

[51] Thomas Alsop. Broadcom's market share semiconductor revenue worldwide from 2010 to 2021. *Statista*. 29 April 2022. Broadcom semiconductor market share 2021 | Statista

[52] Thomas Alsop. Semiconductor revenue market share of Texas Instruments worldwide 2008-2021. *Statista*. 29 April 2021. Texas Instruments semiconductor market share 2021 | Statista

U.S. VS. CHINA: SHARE OF GLOBAL SEMICONDUCTOR MANUFACTURING

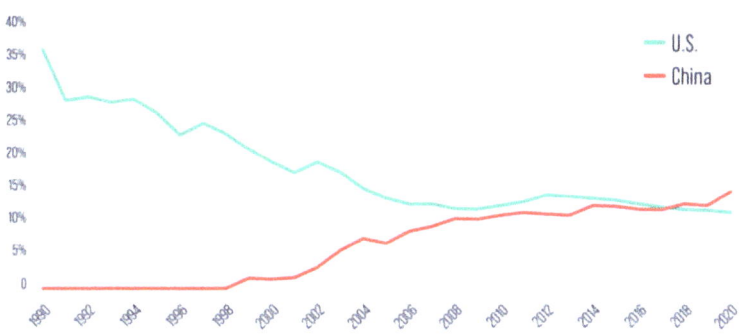

GLOBAL SEMICONDUCTOR FABRICATION CAPACITY 2019

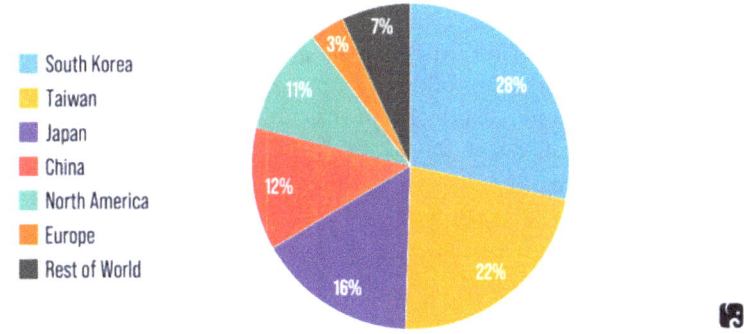

SOURCE: U.S. Senate Republican Policy Committee. Semiconductors: Key to Economic and National Security. Senate RPC. 29 April 2021. Semiconductors: Key to Economic and National Security (senate.gov)

What are Algorithms?

The *Merriam-Webster Dictionary* defines 'algorithms' as "*a procedure for solving a mathematical problem in a finite number of steps that frequently involves repetition of an operation.* Broadly" "*a step-by-step procedure for solving a problem or accomplishing some end.*" Algorithms are usually proprietary computations or a set of rules or a process followed by a computer (machine) in calculations for problem-solving operations. All computer search engines, including Bing, Dogpile Search, Duck Duck Go Search, Google, and Yahoo, use their proprietary algorithms.

The are numerous types of algorithms, normally paired with another word that specifies the type of procedure that will be followed for problem-solving. For example, a "*search*" algorithm refers to a process that will be used to retrieve information from a database. An algorithm consists of adequate, unambiguous finite instructions to produce the desired result. Regardless of the programming language used, algorithms have a common construct, using a step-by-step way of accomplishing their intended purpose. Algorithms have to be designed correctly – with logical steps to be followed – to achieve the desired outcome. In other words, the instructions have to be practical, and the process used stops once the best solution or answer is found, i.e., an output is reached.

A typical algorithm breaks down the problem that it is designed to solve into subproblems and finds the best possible solution most efficiently. The speed of finding a solution is dependent on the speed of the processor being used. The speed of completing the task assigned is also dependent on the complexity and the number of steps required to complete the execution of the algorithm.[53] [54]

What are Biometrics?

Biometrics are '*physical*' and '*behavioral*' identifiers that can be used to recognize an individual using any metrics related to human features. There are about ten identifiers that are currently used to digitally detect the identity of an individual, including electronic fingerprints, facial patterns, voice, and type of cadence or accent. Behavioral identifiers include such things as *keystroke dynamics,* how a person uses a computer mouse, gait, and other patterns of

---

[53] What is an Algorithm? Algorithm Basics. 17 January 2023. What is Algorithm | Introduction to Algorithms – GeeksforGeeks

[54] Kolade Chris. What is an Algorithm? Algorithm Definition for Computer Science Beginners. Free Code Camp. 13 December 2022. What is an Algorithm? Algorithm Definition for Computer Science Beginners (freecodecamp.org)

behavior.[55] [56] [57] Once stolen, biometric data is _compromised for the life of the individual_. U.S. legislation does not restrict the flow of data out of the country, and there is no single, comprehensive Federal law regulating the collection and use of biometric data.

Types of Biometrics

There are three principal types of biometrics: _behavioral, biological,_ and _morphological_. Another school of thought sees two types of biometrics categories, _physiological_ and _behavioral_. There are multiple behavioral patterns of any individual that can be captured by AI, including patterns of typing, way of walking, handwriting, voice patterns, foreign accents, lip motion, and multiple other ways in which people function. Biological biometrics are tied to physical aspects of anyone's biology, such as the size of ears, eye color, height, skin tone, and all body parts. Morphological biometrics include such things as handwriting, gait, and patterns of typing. The most commonly used types of biometrics at this time are electronic fingerprints, photo and video, iris recognition, hand geometry, physiological recognition voice, signature, behavioral characteristics, and DNA. Suppliers of biometric technology are starting to embed behavioral characteristics into their products. These include such things as typing patterns, physical movements, navigation patterns, and engagement patterns. According to current literature on the subject, there are at least twenty-one types of biometrics.[58] Historically, the two principal biometrics used were fingerprints and photographs, and signature recognition, followed by iris recognition, but the list has expanded and continues to expand to previously unthinkable areas.

DNA is another modality of biometric recognition that constitutes its special class. The term stands for _deoxyribonucleic acid_. There is DNA in the nucleus of every cell, and it carries genetic information. It contains units of biological building blocks called nucleotides, with hereditary material in humans, as well as in other organisms.[59] [60]

---

[55] Maria Korolov. What are biometrics? 10 physical and behavioral identifiers that can be used for authentication. _CSOONLINE.com_. 19 February 2019. https://www.csoonline.com/article/3339565/what-is-biometrics-and-why-collecting-biometric-data-is-risky.html

[56] Alexander S. Gillis. Biometrics. https://searchsecurity.techtarget.com. NA. https://searchsecurity.techtarget.com/definition/biometrics

[57] Alison Grace. Biometrics and biometric data: What is it and is it secure? Norton.com. 8 February 2019. https://us.norton.com/internetsecurity-iot-biometrics-how-do-they-work-are-they-safe.html

[58] Robert Smith. 21 Types of Biometrics with Detail Explanation. Biometricstoday.com. 21 Types of Biometrics with Detail Explanation - Biometric Today

[59] What is DNA? Medline Plus. National Library of Medicine. NIH. What is DNA? MedlinePlus Genetics.

[60] Deoxyribonucleic Acid (DNA) Fact Sheet. National Human Genome Research Institute, NIH. Deoxyribonucleic Acid (DNA) Fact Sheet (genome.gov)

DNA has become a key factor to identify suspects and solve crimes by comparing DNA evidence from a crime scene.[61] It can also be used to clear suspects and exonerate individuals mistakenly accused or convicted of crimes. Public crime labs are overwhelmed by backlogs of cases that could be solved by DNA samples collected at crime scenes. Backlogs are due to multiple reasons, but mainly a lack of adequate equipment and trained personnel. AI is increasingly being used to streamline the process of DNA analysis, but the process is still in its infancy.[62]

Biometrics Reliability

The confidence in results achieved using biometrics is limited due to bad *'authenticators"* and technology failures. As with other areas of emerging technology, the legal system governing the use of biometrics and privacy protection differs widely from one jurisdiction to another. Estimates on the efficiency of these systems range from about 86 to 92 percent. According to published estimates, about 62 percent of entities that have a reason to seek the identification of individuals are currently using some form of biometrics, and another 24 percent plan to install and use the technology in the next two years.[63]

- **The top advantages of biometric authentication are** speed of authentication, improved security, increased convenience, scalability, flexibility, higher data accuracy, higher return on investment (ROI), and higher control over access.[64] Other advantages include speedy identification and authentication are convenience, accountability, auditable logs of access to a facility, and increased security over alternative systems.[65]

- **The top disadvantages of biometrics are**: physical disabilities (retina transplants, tattooed hands, and a burnt or damaged finger), software malfunction, scanner issues, systems cannot be accessed 'remotely' to try to

---

[61] Advancing Justice Through DNA Technology: Using DNA to Solve Crimes. U.S. Department of Justice. ADVANCING JUSTICE THROUGH DNA TECHNOLOGY: USING DNA TO SOLVE CRIMES

[62] Using DNA to Solve Crimes. U.S. Department of Justice Archives. ADVANCING JUSTICE THROUGH DNA TECHNOLOGY: USING DNA TO SOLVE CRIMES

[63] Mitek. Advantages and disadvantages of biometrics. Mitek. 15 March 2021. https://www.miteksystems.com/blog/advantages-and-disadvantages-of-biometrics

[64] Top 8 advantages and disadvantages of biometric. *m2sys.com*. 30 May 2020. https://www.m2sys.com/blog/guest-blog-posts/top-8-advantages-and-disadvantages-of-biometric/

[65] Danny Thakkar. Advantages and Disadvantages of Biometric Identification and Authentication. Bayometric.com. https://www.bayometric.com/advantages-disadvantages-biometric-identification/

eliminate sensitive data, fake positives, and potential security breaches by hackers- data stolen could be manipulated to create false positives.[66]

- **Biometric identifiers cannot be changed if compromised.** The biggest disadvantage of biometric identifiers is that if stolen, they cannot be changed (unlike changing a *PIN* or *Password*). Diseases, accidents, and age can cause deterioration of identifiers, and cause a failure to identify an individual. Cost – biometric systems are expensive and technically complex.[67] DOD IT systems, including biometric ID systems, are routinely under attack by individual and state-run adversaries who seek to take advantage of any existing weakness.

- **Biometric vulnerability.** Biometric technology is vulnerable to nefarious actors. An example of a vulnerability is the hacking of the Office of Personnel Management (OPM) in 2015 when the fingerprints of 5.6 million U.S. Government employees were hacked. The government cannot change the fingerprints of individuals whose biometric characteristics were stolen, in the same way, that a stolen password can be replaced.[68] [69]

The growth in the use of biometrics is continuous, progressive, uninterrupted, and pervasive. As the diversity of uses expands, the incentives for hackers to break through biometric security increases. As biometric technology mutates into more sophisticated systems with reduced vulnerabilities, hackers have a more challenging quest to achieve their objectives. Hackers can still break through existing technology to copy and duplicate physical identity features and potentially breakthrough protected barriers. It is increasingly important to update system security software as soon as it becomes available to close vulnerabilities. A physical biometric cannot be transferred or shared digitally – They can only be used with a physical application, i.e., fingerprints, hand geometry, retinal scans, and DNA.[70] [71] U.S.

---

[66] Top 8 advantages and disadvantages of biometric. *m2sys.com*. Op. cit.

[67] Danny Thakkar. Advantages and Disadvantages of Biometric Identification, Op. Cit.

[68] Anuj Sharma. 7 disadvantages of Biometric attendance systems. *Incubsence.com*. 22 March 2020. https://www.incubsence.com/newsroom/7-disadvantages-of-biometric-attendance-systems

[69] Roger A. Grimes. 6 reasons biometrics are bad authenticators [and 1 acceptable use]. CSOonline.com. 4 January 2019. https://www.csoonline.com/article/3330695/6-reasons-biometrics-are-bad-authenticators-and-1-acceptable-use.html

[70] Mitek. Advantages and disadvantages of biometrics. Op. cit.

[71] Danny Thakkar. Advantages and Disadvantages of Biometric Identification, op. cit.

legislation does not restrict the flow of data out of the country.[72] [73] *"In the United States, there is no single, comprehensive federal law regulating the collection and use of biometric data."* [74]

(U) Comparison of Biometric Systems, based on accuracy, cost, devices required and social acceptability

Biometric Technology	Accuracy	Cost	Devices required	Social acceptability
ADN	High	High	Test equipment	Low
Iris recognition	High	High	Camera	Medium-low
Retinal Scan	High	High	Camera	Low
Facial recognition	Medium-low	Medium	Camera	High
Voice recognition	Medium	Medium	Microphone, telephone	High
Hand Geometry	Medium-low	Low	Scanner	High
Fingerprint	High	Medium	Scanner	Medium
Signature recognition	Low	Medium	Optic pen, touch panel	High

(U)Source: http://biometrics.pbworks.com/w/page/14811349/Advantages%20and%20disadvantages%20of%20technologies

---

[72] IIF. Data Flows across Borders: Overcoming Data Localization Restrictions. *Institute of International Finance.* March 2019. https://safe.menlosecurity.com/doc/docview/viewer/docN6E0A8724E4DDe1c67c932b0bc76d740567eee0c592114fbe93ff033efcced96e3c643b76061c

[73] USDOJ. Promoting Public Safety, Privacy, and the Rule of Law Around the World: The Purpose and Impact of the CLOUD Act. U.S. Department of Justice. April 2019. https://www.justice.gov/opa/press-release/file/1153446/download

[74] Thales. Biometric data and privacy laws. (GDPR, CCPA.CPRA). Thales. 16 June 2021. https://www.thalesgroup.com/en/markets/digital-identity-and-security/government/biometrics/biometric-data

Biotechnology

The intersection of biotechnology and AI promises unique synergies, including weaponizing research findings. According to several published reports, China is pushing ethical limits by conducting genetic research on potential engineering and enhancing future soldiers.[75] Genetic engineering research is part of the strategy of military-civilian fusion based on their perception of changes in the character of conflict, and the concept of war for biological dominance. Supercomputing and AI are basic components of this concept for dominance in the future by enhancing 'human performance' through gene-editing technology.

The PLA's Academy of Military Medical Sciences (AMMS) is participating in these efforts. Genetic data from millions of women are being collected for research on population traits, according to a Reuters report. The collected data are being analyzed with AI as part of the effort to gain economic and military advantage.[76] China's concept is to link bioinformatics to seize the strategic commanding heights in the domain of biotechnology as an emerging domain in warfare.[77] [78] AI is being used without ethical considerations for the sake of achieving military dominance.

Medical and Bio-Medical Research

AI is driving fundamental and revolutionary changes in medical and bio-medical research for the analysis of medical data, and in the process, it is changing many aspects of the healthcare sector. It is being used in genetics, epidemiology, clinical virology, microbiology, bioinformatics, diagnostic assistance, data-driven prognostics, statistics, and other aspects of human biology. Through the use of AI, the efficiency of the healthcare system is improving by expediting the processing of information, improving accuracy, reducing costs, increasing efficiency, and improving patient outcomes.

AI is improving the accuracy of the information that clinicians use for more accurate diagnostics. Using *'predictive analytics'* clinicians hope to improve the diagnosis of patients, by predicting the risk of different types of cancer. AI is

---

[75] Elsa B. Kania and Wilson Vorndick. Weaponizing Biotech" How China's Military is Preparing for a 'new domain in warfare.' Defenseone.com. 14 August 2019. Weaponizing Biotech: How China's Military Is Preparing for a 'New Domain of Warfare' - Defense One

[76] Kirsty Needham and Clare Baldwin. Special Report: China's gene giant harvests data from millions of women. Reuters. 7 July 2021. https://www.reuters.com/article/us-health-china-bgi-dna-idUSKCN2ED1A6

[77] Kania and Vorndick, Op. Cite.

[78] Scott Moore. China's Biotech Boom Could Transform Lives – or destroy them. *Foreign Policy*. 8 November 2019. China's Genetic Experiments Are Pushing Ethical Limits (foreignpolicy.com)

helping to identify genetic subtypes, pre-cancerous, and cancerous samples obtained from patients. IA-based tools are important for quality control in multiple areas of medical research. AI has the potential to be more productive, accurate, secure, and impactful in the delivery of medical care to patients.[79] [80] [81] [82] By expediting the analysis of huge amounts of data, AI is helping physicians to make decisions based on experience.

Like the experience in other areas, AI algorithms are not perfectly matching the skills of human doctors, and there are potential risks, possible misdiagnosis, and unintended consequences. However, human doctors can make clinical mistakes, and AI can help them make better decisions. Machine learning does take place, and AI technology learns from mistakes, and in some cases outperforms humans doing so. For example, during the COVID pandemic, AI helped to improve traditional epidemiological tools in an emergency. AI will not replace human physicians but will assist them in their work.[83]

Embedding Chips in Humans

Embedding RFI microchips in humans is not a futuristic science fiction concept. It is already happening for multiple purposes. For example, embedding a 'radio frequency identification chip (RFID) with personal identity, credit card information, a library card, and similar purposes. However, this is only the beginning. Elon Musk is pushing the idea of implanting 'brain chips' in humans, although so far, the U.S. Government has rejected the concept and refused to approve trials of his Neuralink proposal.[84] The Food and Drug Administration (FDA) has not been convinced yet that implanting chips in human brains could result in cures for blindness, paralysis, and other health challenges. The principal problem thus far seems to be linked to questions regarding implanting a lithium battery to power the chips. Questions about animal testing, which has resulted in a large number of monkeys, sheep, pigs, and other test animals are also under review by animal rights organizations.

---

[79] Manu Mitra. Artificial Intelligence in Biomedical Science. *Research Gate*. November 2019.

[80] Rob Matheson (MIT). Automatic artificial intelligence for medical decision-making. *Techplore*. 6 August 2019.

[81] David B. Larson, Giles W. Boland. Imaging Quality Control in the Era of Artificial Intelligence. *National Library of Medicine*, PublMed.gov. 26 June 2019.

[82] Babak Saboury, Michael Morris, and Eliot Siegel. Future Directions in Artificial Intelligence. *National Library of Medicine*, PublMed.gov. November 2021.

[83] Alvin Powell. AI revolution in medicine. *The Harvard Gazette*. 11 November 2020. Risks and benefits of an AI revolution in medicine – Harvard Gazette

[84] Ariel Zilber. Elon Musk's bid to implant chips into human brains shot down by feds. New York Post. 3 March 2023. Feds reject Elon Musk bid to implant chips into human brains (nypost.com)

WHAT IS BIOTECHNOLOGY?

Historically, biotechnology focused on finding food and providing other basic human needs. Early humans focused on such things are finding ways to preserve food. Modern biotechnology is involved with such things are genetic engineering, recombinant DNA technology, modifying bacteria, and other controversial and challenging processes using Artificial intelligence (AI).

Biochemistry
Biostatistics
Cell and Molecular Biology
Computer Science
Engineering
Enzymology
Genetic Manipulation (Animals, bacteria, fungi, plants,)
Immunology
Microbiology
Virology

According to a ruling of the U.S. Patent and Trademark Office published in 2020, <u>AI cannot be an inventor</u>... Only 'natural persons" currently have the right to get a patent. On the other hand, the European Patent Office ruled in 2020 that allows for AI systems to be inventors.

DOES AN INVENTOR HAVE TO BE A HUMAN?

What is Social Media?

Social media is a catch-all term, defined *as computer-based interactive technologies that include digital tools that allow users to create and share content* – including ideas, career interests, and numerous forms of expression, with other members of the public, using a wide range of websites and apps that create virtual communities and networks.[85] The principal social media outlets used by young college students are *Facebook, Twitter,* and *Instagram*. Users of social media can share photos, videos, updates, and links to other internet sites. Social media can result in the misuse of information, and the publication of content that should not be in the public eye. It can also result in identity theft. While some impacts can be positive, they can result in stress, moods, anxiety, emotional insecurities, depression, and addiction. It can be used for making threats, cyberbullying, and promoting violent behavior. It can reduce face-to-face relationships and investment in meaningful activities, and increase sedentary behavior. Undoubtedly, it has helped people to better communicate with others and helped businesses to grow and promote their products and services. There is no consensus as to the impact of social media on an individual's state of mind or lifestyle.[86] [87] [88]

Social media was fueled from the start by the human desire to communicate with other individuals, establish personal links, and nurture these relationships. It has been claimed that social media may have started as far back as 1844, with the invention of the telegraph, and the first message sent from Baltimore to Washington, D.C. by Samuel Morse. More recently, DOD is credited with the start of social media when the Advanced Research Projects Agency Network (ARPANET) was launched in 1969. Others credit the National Science Foundation, as the precursor of the internet was launched as the NSFNET in 1987.[89] With the start of the internet around 1997, the initial communication

---

[85] *Cambridge Dictionary* definition of social media:
Websites and computer programs that allow people to communicate and share information on the internet using a computer or cell phone.
https://dictionary.cambridge.org/us/dictionary/english/social-media

[86] Ekaterina Zhuravskaya, Maria Petrova, and Ruben Enikolopov. Political Effects of the Internet and social media. *Annual Review of Economics*. August 2020.
https://www.annualreviews.org/doi/full/10.1146/annurev-economics-081919-050239

[87] Katie Kennedy. Positive and Negative Effects of social media on Adolescent Wellbeing. Cornerstone-Minnesota State University. 2019.
https://safe.menlosecurity.com/doc/docview/viewer/docN41B59F63072Db0a3b68eb44b38d650e8a359978dd4196a0d17dbd12488071c682f7c53868b0d

[88] Samidh Chakrabarti. Hard Questions: What Effect Does social media Have on Democracy? Facebook. 22 January 2018. https://about.fb.com/news/2018/01/effect-social-media-democracy/

[89] ARPANET was conceptualized as far back as the 1950s. It was founded during the Cold War to build a reliable communications network.

services, CompuServe, America Online, and Prodigy, introduced users to digital communications using email, real-time chatting, and bulletin boards.

LinkedIn came about in 2002, as a network of professionals, and since then it has grown to over 675 million users worldwide.[90][91] After several other starts and stops, Myspace was launched in 2003, which quickly became the most visited website in the world, as it introduced the ability to share music and other content.[92][93] Facebook came about in 2008, and it rapidly took the lead.[94] It was started by Harvard student Mark Zuckerberg. Reddit was launched in 2005, as a news-sharing platform by Steve Huffman and Alexis Ohanian. Twitter was founded in 2006 by Jack Dorsey, Evan Williams, Biz Stone, and others.[95] Instagram was launched in 2010 by Stanford graduate Kevin Systrom as a photo-share site and was later taken over by Facebook. Snapchat was founded in 2011 by Stanford University students Evan Spiegel, Reggie Brown, and Bobby Murphy, concentrating initially on video-sharing services.[96] As of 2021, it was estimated that about 72% of American adults use social media, an estimated 69% are on Facebook, 75% of American adults use Instagram, and about 73% use Snapchat.[97]

---

[90] The History of LinkedIn. https://thelinkedinman.com/history-linkedin/

[91] Erik Gregersen. LinkedIn: American Company. Britannica. 8 July 2021. https://www.britannica.com/topic/LinkedIn

[92] The Editors of Encyclopedia Britannica. Myspace. 4 June 2021. https://www.britannica.com/topic/Myspace

[93] Lori Kozlowski. New Life: How MySpace Spawned A Start-Up Ecosystem. Forbes. 15 May 2012. https://www.forbes.com/sites/lorikozlowski/2012/05/15/how-myspace-spawned-a-startup-ecosystem/?sh=5ef6d42240ba

[94] Andrew Greiner, Seth Fiegerman, Ivory Sherman and Tiffany Baker. Facebook at 15: How a college experiment changed the world. CNN. 1 February 2019. https://www.cnn.com/interactive/2019/02/business/facebook-history-timeline/index.html

[95] Jack Meyer. History of Twitter: Jack Dorsey and the social media Giant. The Street. 18 June 2019. https://www.thestreet.com/technology/history-of-twitter-facts-what-s-happening-in-2019-14995056

[96] Jordan Crook and Anna Escher. A brief history of Snapchat. Techcrunch.com. 15 December 2015. https://techcrunch.com/gallery/a-brief-history-of-snapchat/

[97] Maryville University. The Evolution of social media: How Did it Begin, and Where Could it Go Next. Maryville University. https://online.maryville.edu/blog/evolution-social-media/

Social Media and AI

After a series of startups by young Americans, the Chinese tech company *ByteDance* launched *TikTok* in 2016 and was later merged with *Musically*.[98] It became popular with American young adults and teenagers, and by 2020, it had more than 800 million users worldwide.[99] It did not take long for the U.S. Government to figure out that *TikTok* presented a clear and present danger – or an *immediate security threat*- due to its links to the Chinese Government. As has happened in all areas of IT, social media has been impacted by AI. For example, AI can be used to imitate human behavior and exploit users of social media users. To start with, social media could not exist without the application of AI by the providers of platforms for people to interact with other users, and that can result in numerous forms of abuse. AI can determine the likes and dislikes of social media participants to target them with advertising and entice them to spend. In other words, AI is a very effective marketing tool. AI can also be used to target audiences that may be susceptible to joining political movements and subversive organizations.[100]

In May 2021, a bill to ban *TikTok* on U.S. Government devices passed the Senate Homeland Security and Governmental Affairs Committee unanimously. A similar bill was approved in August 2020, and another bill was introduced in the House of Representatives.[101] Under the Trump Administration, the U.S. Government had approved the sale of the company to an Oracle/Walmart-led group of investors, but the Biden Administration announced in February 2021, that it will not be pushing *TikTok* to sell to a U.S. owner. Another Chinese social media, WeChat, has also been under consideration to be banned in the U.S. for similar concerns.[102] Both of these social media companies are considered Trojan Horses for the Chinese

---

[98] Christina Gayton. The Origins of TikTok. Christinagayton.com. 18 July 2020. https://christinagayton.medium.com/the-origins-of-tiktok-5efa7da4b3e6

[99] ByteDance had about 1.9 billion monthly active users across all its platforms as of December 2020. Source: Liza Lin. TikTok owner ByteDance's annual revenue jumps to $34.3 Billion. Fox News. 17 June 2021.

[100] Desklib. Impact of Artificial Intelligence on social media. 28 October 2022. *Impact of Artificial Intelligence on social media (desklib.com)*

[101] Reuters. Bill to ban TikTok on U.S. Government devices passes committee. Reuters. 12 May 2021. https://www.reuters.com/technology/bill-ban-tiktok-us-government-devices-passes-committee-2021-05-12/

[102] Andrew Hutchinson. US Government Abandons Plans to Force the Sell-Off of TikTok. SocialMediatoday.com. 10 February 2021. https://www.socialmediatoday.com/news/us-government-abandons-plans-to-force-the-sell-off-of-tiktok/594884/

Communist Party, and a security threat to the U.S.[103] DOD issued a warning in December 2019, advising military personnel to delete *TikTok* from all devices due to potential security risks associated with its use.[104]

Is "Social Media' Good or Bad?

Social media is a system designed to interchange information or data, defined as *distinct pieces of information, usually formatted and stored in a way that is related to a specific purpose*.[105] Data is collected for multifold purposes. Data is not necessarily *'factual information,'* even if used for reasoning, discussion, calculation, or to help in decision-making, or information in an electronic form.[106] Like anything else, social media can be used for good and bad. In the hands of perverts of one kind or another, AI-powered social media is a present and increasing danger that is practically impossible to police or regulate.

There are multiple forms of data, including personal or individual data, behavioral data, attitudinal data, and engagement data. It is estimated that, by 2024, the total volume of data created and consumed worldwide will reach 149 zettabytes.[107] (A *'zettabyte'* is a multiple of the unit byte that measures digital storage, and it is equivalent to 1,000,000,000,000,000,000,000 [10^{21}] bytes.[108] The integrity of any analysis based on data depends on the accuracy of the information. Any credible answers resulting from any type of analysis depend on the quality of the data used. Social media distributes data, but readers *do not have a way to accurately judge the accuracy of the information posted in multiple outlets.*

There have been multiple assessments of the consequences of social media use and attempts to determine if the results are good or bad, but there is no

---

[103] Catherine Thorbecke. Republican lawmakers revive efforts to ban TikTok on government devices. ABC News. 15 April 2021. https://abcnews.go.com/Technology/republican-lawmakers-revive-efforts-ban-tiktok-government-devices/story?id=77091017

[104] Mary Meisenzahl. U.S. Government agencies are banning TikTok, the social media app teens are obsessed with, over cybersecurity fears – here's the full list. Businessinsider.com. 25 February 2020. https://www.businessinsider.com/us-government-agencies-have-banned-tiktok-app-2020-2

[105] Webopedia. *Data* refers to distinct pieces of information, usually formatted and stored in a way that is concordant with a specific purpose.

[106] Cambridge Dictionary. https://dictionary.cambridge.org/us/dictionary/english/number

[107] Nemanja Jovancic. 5 Data Collection Methods for Obtaining Quantitative and Qualitative Data. Leadquizzes.com. 10 May 2021. https://www.leadquizzes.com/blog/data-collection-methods/

[108] Max Freedman. How businesses are collecting data (And what they're doing with it). *Businessnewsdaily.com*. 17 June 2020.

consensus.[109] [110] [111] [112] One common finding is that social media use is nearly universal among teenagers. The Pew Research Center reports that 97% of 13-to-17-year-olds use at least one of seven major online platforms, and some spend as long as 9 hours on social media each day. Social media can cause problems when the users cannot determine fiction and reality, is addicting, can be mood-modifying, and it can have mental health consequences. Overuse can cause physical and emotional harm. Suicide rates among 10-to-14-year- have grown more than 50 percent over the last three decades, according to the American Association of 'Suicidology.' In addition, there are multiple cybersecurity issues.

Social Media is a Warzone

Social media is a warzone, and easily exploited to sow confusion, spread false rumors, and distract and distort narratives.[113] There have been numerous documented instances of security breaches of social media platforms, which underscore the vulnerability of the top platforms.[114] From 16-year-olds and bit-time criminals, foreign adversaries, and other nefarious actors have successfully broken into social media platforms. As far back as 2015, jihadist terrorist groups, including Al-Qaeda and ISIS, were communicating using social media to support their conspiracies.[115] Disinformation attacks are frequent. Foreign meddling in the political scene in the U.S. is frequent and has caused numerous violent confrontations, and exploited and promoted social and political divisions in the past three years. Russia, for example, exploited Facebook during the 2016 elections in the U.S., as well as in other countries. Russians have used so-called *sockpuppets*—inauthentic personas on Facebook and elsewhere— to inflame existing political tensions. China likewise, has used a hacking organization

---

[109] Frances Dalomba. Social Media: The Good, The Bad, and The Ugly. Lifespan.org. 3 February 2020. https://www.lifespan.org/lifespan-living/social-media-good-bad-and-ugly

[110] Carrier Clinic. The Good, Bad, and in-between of social media. Carrierclinic.org. 8 August 2019. https://carrierclinic.org/2019/08/08/the-good-bad-and-in-between-of-social-media/

[111] Anna Jolliff. Is social media Good or Bad for Our Mental Health? National Alliance on Mental Illness. 12 August 2020. https://www.nami.org/Blogs/NAMI-Blog/August-2020/Is-Social-Media-Good-or-Bad-for-Our-Mental-Health

[112] Loren Soeiro. Is social media Bad for You? *Psychology Today*. 21 June 2019. https://www.psychologytoday.com/us/blog/i-hear-you/201906/is-social-media-bad-you

[113] L. Gordon Crovitz. Review: social media, Weaponized. *The Wall Street Journal*. 3 December 2017. https://www.wsj.com/articles/review-social-media-weaponized-1512338334

[114] Jason Rivera. Understanding and Countering Nation-State Use of Protracted Unconventional Warfare. Small Wars Journal. 25 October 2014. https://smallwarsjournal.com/jrnl/art/understanding-and-countering-nation-state-use-of-protracted-unconventional-warfare

[115] Yigal Carmon and Steven Stalinsky. Social Media as a National Security Threat. Forbes. 30 June 2015. https://www.forbes.com/sites/realspin/2015/01/30/terrorist-use-of-u-s-social-media-is-a-national-security-threat/?sh=67e66f847619

nicknamed *Spamouflage Dragon* to infect Facebook, YouTube, and Twitter accounts to spread falsehoods and caused violent confrontations during the 2020 elections in the U.S. The FBI and the NCSC have released reports detailing many of these breaches of social media by foreign intelligence agencies.[116] [117] [118] [119]

To reduce vulnerabilities in social media and to encourage the public to practice basic cyber hygiene, the NCSC and the FBI have encouraged the public to practice the following suggestions:[120]

- Never accept an invitation to connect from someone you do not know, even if they are a friend of a friend

- If possible, validate invitation requests through other means before accepting them

- Exercise caution when posting information about yourself, your job, and contacts on social media, as it could draw unwanted attention from adversaries and criminals

- Report suspicious online approaches to appropriate authorities

- Social media has changed how we communicate with each other, the way a large percentage of people get information, and altered how 'reality' is perceived. With the push of a button, an organization or an individual can reach millions of people globally, and cause a crisis overnight. It has become impossible to predict what the next 'big thing' will be. There is no consensus as to the impact of social media on an individual's state of mind or lifestyle. Unhealthy and destructive behaviors are, without a doubt associated with social media addiction. Social media is a warzone.

---

[116] Glenn S. Gerstell. The National-Security Case for Fixing social media. The New Yorker. 13 November 2020. https://www.newyorker.com/tech/annals-of-technology/the-national-security-case-for-fixing-social-media

[117] Timothy N. Whelpley. The Effects of social media on U.S. National Security" (2014). *MSU Graduate Theses*. 1492. Spring 2014. https://bearworks.missouristate.edu/theses/1492/

[118] Social Media and National Security. Thesocialmediamonthly.com 24 February 2020. https://thesocialmediamonthly.com/social-media-and-national-security/

[119] Will Carless. Feds are tracking American's social media to identify dangerous conspiracies. Critics worry for civil liberties. USA Today. 14 May 2021. https://www.usatoday.com/story/news/nation/2021/05/14/terrorist-social-media-narratives-focus-new-dhs-effort/5075237001/

[120] Office of the Director of National Intelligence. Intelligence Threats & Social Media Deception. https://www.dni.gov/index.php/ncsc-features/2780-ncsc-intelligence-threats-social-media-deception

There have been numerous documented instances of security breaches in social media, which underscore the vulnerability of the top platforms. Foreign meddling in the political scene in the U.S. using social media is frequent and has caused numerous violent confrontations, and exploited and promoted social and political divisions in the past three years. Sowing confusion using social media platforms is a documented tactic of Russia and China. The U.S. intelligence community has warned repeatedly about how foreign adversaries are using social media for nefarious purposes. The Office of the Director of National Intelligence has warned that foreign intelligence agencies and criminals routinely use deception on social media platforms. The FBI and the NCSC have released reports to raise awareness of how hostile actors use fake profiles and other forms of deception to target people in government, business, and academia for recruitment and information gathering on a mass scale. The public has been warned to practice basic cyber hygiene when using social media and report suspicious activities to the appropriate authorities.[121]

---

[121] Office of the Director of National Intelligence. *Intelligence Threats & Social Media Deception.* https://www.dni.gov/index.php/ncsc-features/2780-ncsc-intelligence-threats-social-media-deception

Speech Recognition

In plain language, a human speaks, and through AI, a computer recognizes and understands what was said. The first efforts to create machines that could recognize speech go back to 1922, long before the age of computers. Bell Labs by the start of WWII in 1939, had developed technology that allowed machines to recognize a limited number of human sounds. By the early 1950s, Bell Labs had made additional progress, and by 1962, IBM had developed the so-called *Shoebox machine*, able to recognize about a dozen words. By the early 1970s, the U.S. Defense Department created a program funded by the Defense Advanced Research Projects Agency (DARPA) to advance the technology. Within a decade, the technology had been developed to the point that computer software could recognize over 1,000 words. About ten years later, a company named *Nuance Communications*, originally named *Visioneer*, using a Microsoft Windows operating system, issued the first proprietary speech recognition program. By 2000, several leading hardware and software companies were introducing increasingly capable technology with speech recognition capability. With the advent of AI, technology made quantum leaps. As of December 2022, there were multiple "*speech recognition systems*" in the market, including Alexa, Cortana, Siri, and Watson.

Through AI, machines (computers and peripherals) can recognize and process the human voice. *Speech-to-text* software – *transcription* - has been around for at least twenty years, a relatively long time in the computer world. However, innovation continues daily. The technology is also known as natural language processing (NLP). This technology has been embedded or integrated into multiple types of software and is in use by millions who rely on the increasing accuracy of the technology. The market for speech recognition technology is expected to reach $23 billion in 2023. The technology is embedded into telephones, cars, and all kinds of home appliances.

Among the vendors with speech recognition software are: Amazon's *Alexa*, Apple's *Siri*, Google *Assistant*, IBM's Watson, Microsoft's *Cortana and Azure,* and SoundHound's *Hound.* [122] As humans increasingly give verbal commands to these software applications their ability to "think" for themselves is being destroyed. On the other hand, AI is enabling people to make decisions based on efficient analysis of vast amounts of data and experience. [123]

---

[122] Top 5 AI Apps for Speech Recognition. USM. 18 September 2022. Top 5 AI Apps For Speech Recognition | Best AI Apps In 2022 (usmsystems.com)

[123] Op. Cite. Jona Jaupi. Taking Over... 24 December 2022.

Speech Recognition Algorithms

In computer science, an "algorithm" is a process, a set of rules, or rigorous instructions programmed into a computer for problem-solving operations. According to the *Merriam-Webster Dictionary*, an algorithm is *a procedure for solving a mathematical problem...in a finite number of steps that frequently involves the repetition of an operation.* Automatic Speech Recognition (ASR) is the use of algorithms to process human speech into readable text. It can also be used to identify or authenticate the identity of the individual speaking... In other words, through biometric authentication, the identity of a human is made using preconfigured or *"saved voices,"* of the individual.

AI allows computers to use algorithms to recognize and process human speech which starts with digitalizing the sound using software that converts the sound to machine-readable format through digitalization. The technology is also known as *automatic speech recognition* (ASR). It can also go the other way, and transform text into speech. Collecting, and digitalizing speech is not the same as understanding and reacting to the voice data collected.

Computer-Assisted Translation (CAT)

Computer-assisted translation (CAT) is the process of translating a human language into another language through the use of software and a computer. CAT includes a combination of other computer software that includes word processing, spell checkers, and grammar checkers. There are multiple internet-based translation systems available, and an extensive terminology set. Through AI, CAT is producing high-quality translations. Can computer-assisted translator programs currently available as of January 2023 replace a human foreign language translator? Close, but not completely. Computer-assisted translation is increasingly better, but not completely accurate without the text being revised by a human translator.

Machine translation is an automatic process, carried out through the use of AI, using a computer. There are multiple vendors in the market, but *Google Translate* is one of the most powerful and more frequently used. The accuracy of these systems is close to perfection, but it is not quite there yet. Nevertheless, these systems save a lot of time, and when teamed with an expert human translator the results achieved are outstanding. Computer-assisted translation is a more accurate term to describe what can be done with existing software.

Computer-Assisted Interpretation vs Simultaneous Translation

The descriptions and definitions of *"interpretation"* convey a misnomer. In human interpretation, the term indicates *consecutive verbal translation or interpretation from one language to another* while it is being said, or simultaneous interpretation (SI). With the addition of audio headset receivers, smartphones, and computer laptops the process of simultaneous interpretation in real-time is being revolutionized. With modern technology, remote simultaneous interpretation (RSI) is also undergoing a revolution. Through the use of modern equipment, traditional interpreters do not need to be co-located in a conference or meeting, thus reducing associated costs, such as travel. However, humans continue to do the interpretation, not computers using AI. Remote interpretation, including using Webex, MS Teams, or Zoom, continues to use human interpreters. Technology is not able to replace human interpreters in real time.

Foreign Language '*Converters*'

There are multiple examples of software already in the market that can replace human interpreters in real time converting human speech from English to Chinese and vice versa. *Sobolsoft* offers software that has been around since 2012, to translate English to Chinese and vice versa. The results are displayed and can be copied to the clipboard for pasting. It uses *Google Translate* as the backbone for the translations. Accurate voice translations or interpretations are also on the market and work with *iOS* devices and *Android*. The sound is somewhat robotic, but it works. However, it is *blocked in China*! It can only be unblocked with *ExpressVPN*. Why? *iTranslate Converse app.* is another alternative, offering conversational voice translation, but it is not free. It is pricey. Using a cell phone, a screen button is pressed to talk, and the software automatically detects which language is being spoken and provides a super-fast translation. *Microsoft Translator* provides speech translation and shows the translation in Chinese characters or English, depending on which way the translation is going. This software is not blocked by the Chinese Government. Using this system, several phones can be linked using a code, allowing several people to participate in the same conversation. The best feature is that it is freely available. Several similar apps are available from Chinese companies, including *Baidu Translate* and *Huayiwang Translation*. Simultaneous interpretation exists and is in wide use, using accurate results at the same rate of speed as the speaker.

All of these AI-based systems allow a person to speak English or Chinese on a cell telephone and have it immediately translated. They all use an internet connection for voice translation. The Chinese Government controls the use of this technology, but in the U.S. and other countries, there are no controls. Chinese intelligence services have an advantage over competing intelligence services. If the Chinese Government lacks controls, as is the case with *Google Translate*, they block its use in China.

AI-based Cybersecurity

The protection of Information Systems (cybersecurity) is a top national security priority, and the fifth operational domain, after land, air, sea, and space.[124] [125] Critical infrastructure, such as power plants and fuel pipelines have to be protected from advanced hackers who target all vulnerabilities in information systems. Operations in cyberspace are as prevalent as in physical space. Zero-trust networks that incorporate AI are a national defense priority.[126] AI is considered the 4th Industrial Revolution. [127] The U.S. National Security Council (NSC) has been designated as the organization responsible for coordinating the National Cyber Strategy. Gaining and maintaining superiority in cyberspace is critical for defending critical infrastructure, such as fuel pipelines and electric energy networks, deliver strategic and operational advantages to all branches of the military services. AI-based cybersecurity is a basic component of coercive strategies to defend against attack, as well as to deter enemies from taking offensive actions. Military superiority in the air, land, sea, and space is increasingly dependent on defensive and offensive weaponized AI.[128]

---

[124] U.S. Department of Energy. Cyber Security is National Security. Energy.gov. 5 October 2020. Cyber Security is National Security | Department of Energy. Cyber Security is National Security | Department of Energy

[125] GAO. Ensuring the Cybersecurity of the Nation. U.S. Government Accountability Office. Ensuring the Cybersecurity of the Nation (gao.gov)

[126] Andrew Eversden. Pentagon's top IT official: More coordination needed on weapon systems and critical infrastructure cybersecurity. C4ISRNET. 30 June 2021. Pentagon's top IT official: More coordination needed on weapon systems and critical infrastructure cybersecurity (c4isrnet.com)

[127] Gloria Shkuti Ozdemir. Artificial Intelligence Application in the Military: The Case of United States and China. SETA. June 2019. 51_AI_Military.pdf (setav.org)

[128] DOD. Electromagnetic Spectrum Superiority Strategy. Department of Defense. October 2020. DoD Electromagnetic Spectrum Superiority Strategy 2020 (nps.edu)

More Tools for Cyber Criminals

Just about anything powered by AI can be weaponized by cybercriminals and a wide assortment of nefarious actors, including rogue states. The threats are real, and as AI becomes more sophisticated, they become even more dangerous. There are no ethical concerns in the highly disruptive transformative technology revolution. It is increasingly difficult to detect, monitor, or control what can be done with AI. The following are some of the latest examples that have been recently added to the dilemmas associated with AI.

AI to Mimic the Human Voice

In January 2023, Microsoft announced another AI product, *VALL-e*, capable of mimicking a human voice after only listening to three seconds of speech.[129] Cybercriminals have been using this type of AI tool for at least two years, to impersonate a person's relative with a false story, which requires money desperately to solve, such as an arrest for drunk driving. This Microsoft product can turn written text into speech, mimicking the voice of any individual, thus enabling criminal elements to expand scams with an even better tool, including the emotional, tonal, and pacing range of the voice of an individual.

Google Voice has been around for some time and has been frequently used by scammers for identity theft. People need to be on guard anytime anyone calls demanding information.[130] Fraud using voice software is rampant. Particularly, if a caller uses high-pressure tactics, and urges fast action.[131] For example, *extended warranty scams* for cars happen all the time. A serious warning by Google and other software companies is NEVER give a stranger any information, particularly any type of computer code. Scammers capitalize on any information

---

[129] Ciaran Daly. Terrifying Microsoft AI can build a robo-clone of your voice after just 3 seconds. *Daily Star*. 11 January 2023. Terrifying Microsoft AI can build a robo-clone of your voice after just 3 seconds - Daily Star

[130] Federal Trade Commission. The Google Voice scam: How this verification code scam works and how to avoid it. U.S. Federal Trade Commission. 29 October 2021. The Google Voice scam: How this verification code scam works and how to avoid it | Consumer Advice (ftc.gov)

[131] Charlotte Hilton Andersen. What Is the Google Voice Scam, and How Can You Avoid it? *Reader's Digest*. 26 October 2022. Google Voice Scams: How They Work and How to Protect Yourself (rd.com)

they can obtain from victims using a wide variety of tricks. Never fall for offers and deals that seem too good to be true... *They are not true!* [132] [133] [134]

ChatBot or Chatterbot – What is it?

Computer programs supported by AI and designed for computers to converse or interact with humans coherently over the internet are called '*chatbot.*' They can use simulated human conversation (natural language processing NLP), or use text and/or graphics. These programs have existed for many years, and their use continues to grow, as the public becomes more accustomed to and tolerant of customer service automation. As time passes, more types of chatbots emerge, and they become more effective in understanding and answering queries from humans. For the exam, the technology is increasingly able to understand the emotions of humans, predict behavior, and provide personalized answers. This technology reduces costs for companies and is becoming more acceptable to customers, who increasingly are faced with only one choice, either interacting with a computer or not obtaining whatever they are seeking, because it is impossible to talk to a real person.

ChatGPT -a Godsend or a Hex?

In November 2022, a new '*generative pre-trained transformer*' or '*AI chatbot*' developed by OpenAI named ChatGPT, was introduced to the Internet. According to '*open source*' reporting, '*ChatGPT,*' uses AI to '*help*' students cheat on assigned homework, but cybercriminals and other nefarious actors immediately became users.[135] Details spread through social media among students in high schools and colleges in several countries. The app can write convincingly human answers to questions, and produce term papers based on specific questions and classroom assignments. It works similarly to a search tool, such as *Yahoo* or *Google*. However, the AI-powered app not only searches for information, but it

---

[132] Government of Massachusetts. Google Voice Scams. Mass.gov. 8 December 2022. "Google Voice" Scams | Mass.gov

[133] Patrick J. Kiger. 7 Top Scams to Watch Out for in 2023. *AARP*. 4 January 2023. Here Are 7 Top Scams You Should Watch Out for in 2023 (aarp.org)

[134] Jim Akin. How to Recognize and Avoid Google Voice Scams. *Experian*. 8 October 2022. How to Recognize and Avoid Google Voice Scams – Experian

[135] Note: ChatGPT is owned by OpenAI, which also produces Vall-E and GitHub Copilot, which generate computer code using AI. OpenAI Inc. is a non-profit AI research and deployment company. Microsoft is a key investor. The company was founded in 2015 in San Francisco by Sam Altman, Elon Musk, Peter Thiel, Reid Hoffman, Jessica Livingston, and others.

can also *'write'* an essay on a given subject, mimicking a human author. [136] [137] [138] *How obscene is this application of AI?*

Some student entrepreneur *'geniuses'* used their computer knowledge to go into business selling their know-how of *ChatGPT* to produce homework assignments for other students. The potential impact on education and society as a whole by the misuse of AI technology could be very serious. Nevertheless, it may also have the opposite result, getting students to pay attention and possibly increase their knowledge of the subject of the assigned school work. There are all kinds of moral issues with this entire experience, but that is one of the key points of AI, *it has no morals or ethics.* [139] Some creative teachers are using the ChatGPT controversy as a *'teaching moment.'* For example, a fifth-grade teacher is using ChatGPT as a teaching tool, and educate his students on the pros and cons of AI, and challenging them to compete in a writing game against the computer.[140]

Experimentation with the new app spread fast. University of Minnesota law professors used ChatGPT to generate answers to four law school exams, and while humans averaged a B+, ChatGPT averaged a C+. The AI-empowered system got a 'passing grade,' but did not excel, despite being considered the top-rated example of generative intelligence. The areas tested included *"Constitutional Law, Employee Benefits, Taxation, and Torts."* ChatGPT performed poorly at multiple choice questions involving math but performed better on essays. The professors were able to figure out which exams were written by AI machines and which were written by humans. [141] Another first was scored by Congressman Jake Auchincloss (D.- Mass) on 25 January 2023, when he delivered a speech in the House of Representatives that was written using ChatGPT, on the subject of a

---

[136] AFP. AI, do my homework! How ChatGPT pitted teachers against tech. *France Agence Press.* 18 January 2023. AI, do my homework! How ChatGPT pitted teachers against tech | Tech News (hindustantimes.com)

[137] KCCI. Educators worry new tech tool could essentially do students' homework for them. *KCCI Des Moines.* 16 January 2023. Educators worry ChatGPT could essentially do students' homework for them (kcci.com)

[138] Greg Rosalsky, Emma Peaslee, Brittany Cronin, and Kate Concannon. Did AI write this headline? *NPR.* 18 January 2023. Was this text written by ChatGPT artificial intelligence? : The Indicator from Planet Money : NPR

[139] Katie Wickens. Even an AI thinks using AI to write your homework is a bad idea. *PCGamer.* 28 September 2022. Even an AI thinks using AI to write your homework is a bad idea | PC Gamer

[140] Jocelyn Gecker. Amid ChatGPT outcry, some teachers are inviting AI to class. AP News. 13 February 2023. Amid ChatGPT outcry, some teachers are inviting AI to class | AP News

[141] Sophie Mann. Not as smart as we thought: ChatGPT averaged a C+ when University of Minnesota law professors used it to generate answers in four law-school exams - while humans averaged a B+. Daily Mail. 26 January 2023. ChatGPT averaged a C+ when law professors used it to generate answers to law school exams | Daily Mail Online

bill that would create a joint U.S.-Israel Artificial Intelligence Center. The proposed law would create a joint center that would serve as a hub for AI research.[142]

For every problem, there is a solution. Schools have been forced to come up with algorithms to instruct AI-powered apps to determine if a term paper or any other homework has been plagiarized using an AI application, such as *ChatGPT*. One of the *'antidotes'* is called *GPTZero*, empowered by AI to analyze a paper and determine if it was written by an *'intelligent machine.'* Someone thought of the idea of asking AI if it is proper to use AI to provide students with their homework. The AI-powered machine answered back that it was not such a good idea... Perhaps AI can determine when something is a scourge that can poison the minds of students, despite having no morals or ethics. There is never a dull moment when it comes to AI!

The concept behind ChatGPT is not going away, according to press reports, Microsoft is investing billions in chatbot maker OpenAI. According to press reports, Microsoft management, AI will continue to grow in the future and has the potential to revolutionize many economic sectors. Google, which has the leading search engine, apparently is concerned that OpenAI and Microsoft could wrestle market share in the search engine business. Almost immediately after its release, there were comments all over the Internet about the possibility that ChatGPT could be used to generate malware and write phishing emails by bad criminal elements and all kinds of bad actors.[143] It did not take long for cybercriminals to use ChatGPT to rip off individuals and organizations. The app is already being used to generate phishing emails and malicious code for malware attacks.[144]

Microsoft 'Bing' and Google 'Bard'

Despite the participation of Microsoft in the funding of ChatGPT, the company created its version of a similar AI program named Bing and started marketing it around January 2023. Microsoft built Bing in partnership with OpenAI, the company behind ChatGPT. Using AI, this software can answer search the web and answer questions posed by users, mostly geared for consumer questions, such as *"Help me create a trivia quiz,' 'How do I pick the*

---

[142] Steve LeBlanc. Member of Congress reads AI-generated speech on the House floor. *AP News*. 26 January 2023. Member of Congress reads AI-generated speech on House floor | AP News

[143] Bloomberg. What should you think about ChatGPT> Ask some humans? *Bloomberg*. 29 June 2023.

[144] Hannah Getahun. It's not just for you: Cybercriminals are also using ChatGPT to make their jobs easier. *Insider*. 24 February 2023. It's not just you: Cybercriminals are also using ChatGPT to make their jobs easier (yahoo.com)

best dog breed for me? Is it better to adopt or buy?' 'What art ideas can I do with my kid?' It is marketed as a way to conduct a 'chat' naturally and ask follow-up questions and get AI-generated personalized replies. Bing works with the Microsoft Edge browser. Reviewers have pointed out that in the past decade, Google dominated the search engine market, with about 86.6 percent share of the global search market, as compared to Microsoft search engine with about 6.7 percent market share, but is trying to attract new users with Bing, incorporated into the Edge web browser. Google also issued its AI-empowered chat named 'Bard.' ChatGPT, Bing, and Bard have similar advantages and disadvantages, weir results, and controversies.[145] [146] [147]

Video *Deepfakes* and *Synthetic Media*

With the use of AI technology, phony hyper-realistic videos and audio recordings of people, who look and sound just like real individuals. A frequently used tool is TikTok, a Chinese product of a company named ByteDance.[148] AI-based programs manipulate media using artificial neural networks, autoencoders, and machine learning techniques to produce fake videos. These videos can be used by criminal elements to extort money from victims, or by all kinds of nefarious actors to confuse the public and possibly cause all kinds of social disturbances, and national security threats. Photorealistic media has the potential to cause very serious consequences. Some people view these manipulations as fun, but they are not, because they have a dark side to them.

The possibilities for wrongdoing are huge, from generating fake pornography to incidents that could trigger street violence, rogue actors can manufacture fake videos that can be used to manipulate social media and cause significant upheavals by making victims sound and look as if they were making vile comments, participating in atrocities, or committing illegal acts. To start with, audiovisual evidence can no longer be regarded as legitimate. Detecting forgeries has also been born with the advent of deepfakes. As Sir Isaac Newton stated in his Third Law: of Motion, *for every action, there is always an equal and*

---

[145] Clare Duffy. I tried Microsoft's new AI-powered Bing. Here's what it's like. *CNN Business*. 8 February 2023. I tried Microsoft's new AI-powered Bing. Here's what it's like – CNN

[146] Michael Muchmore. ChatGPT and 15 Other Reasons to Drop Google for Microsoft's Bing. *PC Magazine*. 9 February 2023. ChatGPT and 15 Others Reasons to Drop Google for Microsoft's Bing | PCMag

[147] Winston Burton. Google vs Microsoft Bing: A Detailed Comparison of Two Search Engines. *Search Engine Journal*. 2 April 2021. Google vs Bing: A Detailed Comparison of Two Search Engines (searchenginejournal.com)

[148] Peter Suciu. TikTok's Deepfakes Just the Latest Security Issue for the Video Sharing App. *Forbes*. 7 January 2020. TikTok's Deepfakes Just the Latest Security Issue for The Video Sharing App (forbes.com)

opposite or contrary, reaction. Authentication schemes are entering the market to counteract the impact of fake media.[149]

For example, Microsoft announced a new *Video Authenticator* to identify deepfakes in September 2020. The new technology can detect manipulated content and verify the authenticity of videos. The technology was built by Microsoft Research and Microsoft Azure, in partnership with the Defending Democracy Program.[150] However, there is a push-pull reaction to AI technology, and so far, all the predictions of doomsday have not materialized and so far, a deepfake apocalypse has not materialized.[151] [152]

Voice Deepfakes are also increasingly being used by all kinds of nefarious actors as of February 2022. The voices of world leaders have been copied and altered with AI technology to produce fake audio clips. Cybercriminals are using the technology to call people using a relative's speech pattern to request assistance to recover from fake incidents, such as asking for money to get bailed out of jail after a fake traffic incident, and numerous other fake situations.[153]

Personal Privacy: A Thing of the Past

With the introduction of several subsets of AI, personal privacy has been disappearing at an alarming rate. Just about every economic sector, financial institutions, banks, hotel chains, airlines, cruise companies, insurance companies, software companies, and government agencies at all levels are collecting personal information. Privacy is practically nonexistent anymore. Members of the European Union (EU) tried unsuccessfully to protect the privacy of their population.[154] The issue became practically a daily source of friction between the EU and the U.S., as there has never been a serious attempt to legislate protection for people's right to privacy. The idea that privacy is a human

---

[149] M. Mitchell Waldrop. Synthetic media; The real trouble with deepfakes. *Knowable Magazine.* 16 March 2020. Synthetic media: The real trouble with deepfakes (knowablemagazine.org)

[150] Tom Burt. New Steps to Combat Disinformation. Microsoft. 1 September 2020. New Steps to Combat Disinformation - Microsoft On the Issues

[151] Matteo Wong. We Haven't Seen the Worst of Fake News. *The Atlantic.* 20 December 2022. It's Time to Worry About Deepfakes Again - The Atlantic

[152] Eric Horvitz. On the Horizon: Interactive and Compositional Deepfakes. *Cornell University.* 5 September 2022. [2209.01714] On the Horizon: Interactive and Compositional Deepfakes (arxiv.org)

[153] Chris Stoked-Walker. Voice Deepfakes Of Everyone From Joe Rogan to Joe Biden Are Taking Over Social Media. *Buzzfeednews.* 28 February 2023. Voice Deepfakes Of Celebs Are Taking Over Social Media (buzzfeednews.com)

[154] In 2018, the EU enacted the General Data Protection Regulation (GDPR), but by then it was too little and too late.

right did not gain real support from political leaders. Personal space is pretty much gone like the dinosaurs. Just about everything now is public. Not until a person is hacked, and personal financial losses occur, is the issue put on the front burner. All the ethical considerations that existed before the advent of social media are a thing of the past. Mass surveillance is now a fact of life. [155] [156] [157] [158] [159] These are some examples of how privacy has been torpedoed by several private sector programs in the past twenty years:

Affinity Credit Cards

The so-called '*affinity credit card*' is credit card offered in conjunction with two organizations, the bank or institution that issues the card, and a non-Bank or nonfinancial organization with which consumers have an affinity. An affinity is a liking of something, for example, universities, sports franchises, nonprofit organizations, and airline companies, with a credit card. A wide variety of organizations use affinity cards as a way of obtaining financial support from their members. The physical feature of these cards is that they carry a form of advertising for the institution or business, and entices cardholders to use them. The banking institutions that issue the credit cards pay their partners' set fees for every new member that is issued a card, a commission every time the card is used, a small percentage of annual fees, and a share of interest paid by the card holders. The airlines, receive funds painlessly without any financial exposure. The financial institutions benefit because they obtain loyal customers, in a very competitive credit card environment. In the process, banking institutions collect a tremendous amount of personal information and share or sell the information to other entities. For all practical purposes, U.S. credit card holders can't prevent their personal information from being shared or sold to multiple partners of

---

[155] Paul Wagenseil. Your Privacy is Gone. You Just Don't know it Yet. *Tom's Guide*. 31 July 2017. Your Privacy Is Gone. You Just Don't Know It Yet | Tom's Guide (tomsguide.com)

[156] Christian Zilles. Social Media and the Death of Personal Privacy. Socialmediahq.com 22 October 2018. Social Media and The Death of Personal Privacy (socialmediahq.com)

[157] James Brusseau. What to do When Privacy is Gone. *Old Dominion University*. 29 May 2019. "What to Do When Privacy Is Gone" by James Brusseau (odu.edu)

[158] Peter Sucio. There Isn't Enough Privacy on Social Media and That is a Real Problem. *Forbes*. 26 June 2020. There Isn't Enough Privacy on Social Media and That Is A Real Problem (forbes.com)

[159] Ramesh Raskar. Apps Gone Rogue: Maintaining Personal Privacy in an Epidemic. *DeepAI*. 19 March 2020. Apps Gone Rogue: Maintaining Personal Privacy in an Epidemic | DeepAI

financial institutions issuing the cards.[160] [161] The companies participating in these schemes, share card-holder information, for example:

- Name of the cardholder, address, phone, employment, annual income...
- Credit score...
- What the credit card is used for, including items purchased, and where...
- Personal travel information, including travel patterns, preferred carriers...
- The Hotel chains normally used by cardholders...
- Family members sharing a credit card account...

Frequent Flyer Programs

Since their inception in the early 1980s, *'frequent flyer programs'* have *'morphed'* constantly, and members have faced frequent changes in redemption rates, perks, and rewards programs. Transparency is not a key feature of these programs. The research company J.D. Power, an expert in measuring customer satisfaction conducted a study of airline loyalty programs from the largest U.S. air carriers. They found that the airlines have made so many alterations to their frequent flier programs that nearly half of all consumers do not fully understand how to redeem their mileage points in ways that would yield the most satisfying results.[162] The frequent flyer programs, despite the questionable level of member satisfaction with the perks, are money-makers for the airlines. The profitability is no longer linked to the number of miles flown by members but by commissions generated by *'affinity credit cards'* linked to the *'frequent flyer programs,"* and other similar arrangements by which the total purchasing practices of the members generate income for the airlines.

Financial institutions and their travel sector programs collect a considerable amount of information on individuals. Basic demographic information includes name, nationality, birth date, address, phone number, and in many cases employer or work location, purchase history, travel frequency, locations, preferences, credit history, where they normally shop, frequently used

---

[160] Jay Stanley. Why Don't We Have More Privacy When We Use A Credit Card? ACLU.13 August 2019. https://www.aclu.org/blog/privacy-technology/consumer-privacy/why-dont-we-have-more-privacy-when-we-use-credit-card

[161] Burt Helm. Credit card companies are tracking shoppers like never before: inside the next phase of surveillance capitalism. *Fast Company*. May/June 2020 issue of Fast Company magazine. https://www.fastcompany.com/90490923/credit-card-companies-are-tracking-shoppers-like-never-before-inside-the-next-phase-of-surveillance-capitalism

[162] Dan Reed. Frequent Flier Programs Are Now More About Raking In Revenue Than Pleasing Top Customers. *Forbes*. 7 November 2019. https://www.forbes.com/sites/danielreed/2019/11/07/frequent-flier-programs-invented-to-drive-customer-loyalty-are-now--more-about-raking-in-more-revenue-than-pleasing-top-customers/?sh=69d3da8a15b3

IP computer addresses, and other trivial information. However, when aggregated, the data form a very complete picture of individual behavior. Biometrics, including facial recognition technology (FRT) data, are increasingly being collected and added to individual profiles of both, "*affinity credit card*" holders, and "*frequent flyer*" program participants. In addition to these information-sharing efforts, biometrics have been increasingly added to the mix. These are some examples:

Facial Recognition Technology (FRT)

As previously covered, FRT is the "*automatic collection and processing of digital images which contain people's faces for identification, authentication, verification, or categorization of individuals* using *"physiological characteristics."* This intrusive surveillance technology is ubiquitous in airports and other transportation hubs, government office buildings, schools, banks, casinos, shopping malls, and other key sites where security is important.

Typical Airline Kiosk

At the US National Institute of Standards and Technology (NIST), a total of 262 algorithms from more than 150 developers were evaluated in January 2021. China has cornered the FRT surveillance markets worldwide, and by 2018, it accounted for nearly half of the global market.[163] With increased global interconnectivity, FRT manufacturers may be receiving and collecting data from their customers, and creating huge databases that may be shared with nefarious intelligence agencies. FRT-derived information provides "*puzzle pieces*" to adversaries seeking "*patterns of life*" for DOD civilian and uniformed personnel and their families as they travel internationally. FRT is a *de facto* weapon for strategic intelligence collection with little if any accountability. Progressively, the FRT data collected is fed into '*affinity credit card*' and "*frequent flyer*" programs. Personal privacy becomes a thing of the past as these programs become interlinked. And how is all of this biometric data collected and disseminated? Let's start with airline kiosks at airports.

Airline kiosks are devices that allow passengers to self-check in, pay fees with credit and debit cards, and check-in luggage. Touch-screen kiosks are being replaced with '*no-touch screen devices,*' that use biometrics to screen

---

[163] Yuan Yang and Madhumita Murgia. How China cornered the facial recognition surveillance market. *Los Angeles Times.* 9 December 2019. https://www.latimes.com/business/story/2019-12-09/china-facial-recognition-surveillance

passengers.[164] [165] The technology allows for minimal face-to-face contact between passengers and airport and airline employees and reduces the possibility of contamination from most diseases, including COVID-19.

The vulnerability of this technology to hackers is not unlike the exposure of airline loyalty programs, and credit and debit card systems. Just about any system can potentially be spoofed. The fact that the kiosks are newer and more advanced does not necessarily assure that they are impenetrable. These systems use cookies to *'enhance user experience,'* but the passengers do not have a real choice about being tracked by them.[166] The kiosks automatically receive and record private information from passengers using a variety of methods to process personal information, and the information is stored and shared with multiple business partners. Normally Customs and Immigration authorities from the originating country and the destination country are provided collected information from the passengers, i.e., nationality, passport number, country of birth, address, names of relatives traveling together, and flight information.

The COVID-19 pandemic has accelerated the deployment of advanced biometric technologies to reduce human contact at airports by increasingly relying on electronic identification. From the moment a traveler checks into a flight at an airport kiosk, personal data is collected, processed, stored, and shared with multiple parties. Increased data collection and data analysis on individuals has significantly reduced personal privacy. The traveling public has very little if any choice to opt out of the multiple systems of collection of personal information. Ubiquitous surveillance is the new reality in the travel sector. The extracted personal information from travelers can be used for 'predictive analytics' using artificial intelligence (AI) for marketing products and services, based on likes and dislikes, purchasing habits, income, credit rating, and other factors.

Luggage Tags

Luggage tags are a form of identification for suitcases used by travelers on cruise ships, trains, and airplanes. They help passengers identify their bags upon arrival at their destination in baggage carousels, help to prove the ownership of a piece of luggage, and for tracking missing baggage. Travel security experts recommend that travelers do not put American flags on luggage, and

---

[164] Robert Silk. Carriers rush to deploy contactless tech in airports. *Travel Weekly.* 22 June 2020. https://www.travelweekly.com/Travel-News/Airline-News/Carriers-rush-to-deploy-contactless-tech-in-airports

[165] Adele Berti. The rise of touchless technology at airports. *Airport Technology.* 17 September 2020. https://www.airport-technology.com/features/touchless-technology-airports/

[166] Katherine Lagrave. How Airlines and Airports Use Your Data, From Security to the Flight Itself. Traveler. 28 August 2019. https://www.cntraveler.com/story/how-airlines-and-airports-use-your-data-from-security-to-the-flight-itself

limit the information on the tags to name, phone number, and perhaps an email address. They recommend that luggage be marked to make them more visible from a distance and that the same information that is on the tag be placed inside the luggage, in case thieves yank off the tag. They should pack and carry their bags, and know the contents when crossing borders, catching flights, or passing through Customs. They should not offer or accept to carry anything for anyone else. Travelers should make a list of what is inside the checked luggage, if at all possible, take a picture of the contents in case it is stolen, and an insurance claim has to be filed with the air carrier. Travelers should avoid being distracted, complacent, or looking disoriented, particularly around luggage carousels upon arrival at their destination.

In summary, In the environment spawned by the coronavirus pandemic in 2020-2022, traditional data collection, has been enhanced. Data collected through travel and leisure sector programs present significant exposure to hackers, and an assortment of nefarious actors are gaining access to and exploiting information on the traveling public, and assembling the *'puzzle pieces'* to identify *'patterns of life.'* U.S. legislation does not restrict the flow of data out of the country, and there is no single, comprehensive Federal law regulating the collection and use of biometric data and travel sector loyalty programs.

Ubiquitous Technical Surveillance (UTS) with AI

Ubiquitous surveillance can become increasingly difficult to escape with the proliferation of multiple technologies, such as biometrics and its sub-branches, such as facial recognition technology (FRT). Technical surveillance is simply another form of Big Data. AI could be used to sort through the huge amount of data collected through technical surveillance, which includes redundant and irrelevant material, and a considerable amount of junk.[167] Weaponized AI could reduce false positives, and zero in on clear risks before they turn into an actual threat. It has been suggested that there is a need for a counterintelligence analysis cadre to integrate a full range of disciplines to monitor, assess, and share foreign CI threat information, and adapt and respond to increasingly complex threats.[168]

Hyped Brain Wave Monitoring Technology

The weaponization of AI has huge possibilities. It is impossible to figure out what may be around the corner with AI technology, even for *'techies.'* According to a presentation made at the annual World Economic Forum in Davos

---

[167] Iessit. Ubiquitous Surveillance and Security. Technology and Society. 29 June 2017. https://technologyandsociety.org/ubiquitous-surveillance-and-security/

[168] Jacqueline H. Poreda. Intelligence After Next: Building a counterintelligence analytic cadre. *MITRE.* February 2021. https://technologyandsociety.org/ubiquitous-surveillance-and-security/

Switzerland in 2023, *'hyped brain wave monitoring technology'* may be available soon, which would allow an employer to detect what is going through the minds of their employees. Using AI-machine-supported software with enhanced surveillance capabilities, it may be possible to collect and analyze brain-wave activity. Ear pods could be used to figure out what is going on in the brain of an individual. Governments would be able to subpoena data related to the brainwaves of individuals to find out if they are participating in espionage, a fraud scheme, or some other illegal activity. Based on the information that was disclosed at the gathering, MIT and Duke University, as well as other entities, such as Meta, are developing brain monitoring technology.[169]

The human brain produces or emits electrical power, and generates waves of different frequencies, associated with different situations, specific behavior, including emotions, and instructions to other parts of the human body. These waves represent different states of the mind, from high arousal to deep sleep. Scientists have been studying and monitoring all kinds of brain waves as far back as the 1920s, but with the advent of AI, they have been able to make quantum leaps to record and analyze brain waves.[170]

According to articles, AI-supported technology with the ability to decode brainwaves is already available. Such things as emotions and even pre-conscious thought can already be done using AI. What was deemed impossible not long ago, is now possible. In addition to all the other existing technology to collect, store, and analyze all kinds of personal information, it is now possible to expand surveillance using *'electromyography'* signals to analyze brain signals and figure out any person's thoughts.[171] As far back as 2016, this technology was being developed using AI.[172] There are multiple ethical, legal, and social implications of this technology, which in the wrong hands, could empower all kinds of rogue actors to carry out some very nasty activities. Privacy has been lost. If asked to wear some wearable device at a workplace, or any other venue, think before you accept. A headset, earplugs, helmets, and other devices may be hiding their true purpose. Implanting *'brain-computer interfaces'* (BCI) have already been implanted in volunteers. In China, government-sponsored research has been

---

[169] Allum Bokhari. Davos Globalists Hype Companies Spying on Workers' Brain Waves. *Breitbart.* 3 February 2023. Davos Globalists Hype Companies Spying on Workers' Brain Waves (breitbart.com)

[170] Dr. S.S. Verma. Putting Electronics of Brain Waves to Use. Electronicsforu.com 28 July 2020. Putting Electronics Of Brain Waves To Use | Must Read (electronicsforu.com)

[171] Tim Newcomb. Companies already Have the Ability to Decode Your Brainwaves. *Popular Mechanics.* 24 January 2023. Companies Already Have the Ability to Decode Your Brainwaves (popularmechanics.com)

[172] Simon Torkington. They're already here: devices that let your boss monitor your brain. *World Economic Forum.* 31 October 2016. They're already here: devices that let your boss monitor your brain | World Economic Forum (weforum.org)

using brainwave reading helmets to track workers and monitor their brain activity as far back as 2018, and possibly longer.[173]

Cyber-Exotic Brain-Computer Interface (BCI)

There are multiple exotic ideas in the AI fantasyland that are not completely out of the question. For example, the idea of brain implants and brain-computer interface for mind-controlled computing on human guinea pigs. In other words, individuals with an implanted 'chip' would be able to control and operate technology gadgets only with their minds using their brain blood vessels. People suffering from some form of paralysis may be able to overcome their handicaps using this technology. BCI would incorporate software that mimics the function of the subcortical and spinal mechanisms that participate in normal movement control in humans. One of the prime movers in these projects is Elon Musk, SpaceX, CEO of Tesla, and Twitter. Bill Gates (Microsoft) and Jeff Bezos (Amazon) are also mentioned as investors in the BCI concept. The U.S. Food and Drug Administration (FDA) has already provided approval for experimentation, including trials of BCI. People affected with degenerative diseases may benefit from the technology, but without a doubt, the possibility of weaponizing BCI is always around. *Electrocorticography,* electroencephalograms, *neurofeedback, neuroscience, neuromodulation,* neuroprosthetics, *transcranial magnetic stimulation,* and other related terms are all interrelated now through AI. Science fiction and ethics are not what they used to be.[174] [175] [176] [177] [178]

---

[173] Spooky. Chinese Companies Equip Workers with Brainwave Reading helmets to Increase Productivity. *OddityCentral.* 2 May 2018. Chinese Companies Equip Workers with Brainwave Reading Helmets to Increase Productivity (oddlycentral.com)

[174] Ashley Capoot. Brain implant startup backed by Bezos and Gates is testing mind-controlled computing on humans. *CNBC.* 18 February 2023. Synchron backed by Bezos and Gates tests brain-computer interface (cnbc.com)

[175] Brain-Computer Interface. *Science Direct.* Brain-Computer Interface - an overview | ScienceDirect Topics

[176] Jonathan R. Wolpaw, José del R. Millán, Nick F. Ramsey. Brain-computer interfaces: Definitions and principles. National Library of Medicine. Brain-computer interfaces: Definitions and principles - PubMed (nih.gov)

[177] Rashad Safir. Brain-Computer Interfaces: Everything you need to know. Brain-Computer Interfaces: Everything you need to know | by Rashad Safir | TechTalkers | Feb, 2023 | Medium

[178] Laura Y. Cabrera and Douglas J. Weber. Rethinking the ethical priorities for brain-computer interfaces. Nature Electronics. 15 February 2023. Rethinking the ethical priorities for brain–computer interfaces | Nature Electronics

Mitigation Strategies to Reduce Exposure to Bad Actors

Cybercriminals and state intelligence organizations use stealth methods to gain access to computer networks. They use cutting-edge technology, increasingly assisted by AI to achieve their goals. The National Security Agency (NSA) issued a list of ten mitigation actions that assist in reducing exposure to bad actors. Weaponized AI can more efficiently apply these techniques to accomplish more advanced defense-in-depth security to mitigate the tactics of cybercriminals. The key cybersecurity functions that can be enhanced with AI are: identifying, protecting, detecting, responding, and recovering.[179]

To the extent possible, all network connections should be encrypted, and all emails should be filtered to delete spam and reduce phishing attacks. When in doubt, do not open emails that are suspected of containing malware, and simply delete them. As soon as a new version of the software is released, download it, because without a doubt it will have patches to correct prior weaknesses to hacking. Cybercriminals are always on the lookout and surveilling for vulnerabilities. These criminals use what is called *'Advanced Persistent Threat'* (APT) to target vulnerabilities and disrupt computer systems. State-sponsored intelligence operations resemble the actions of intruders to find open backdoors to gain access to databases and infiltrate networks.[180] Web application firewalls and antivirus programs are critical to prevent intrusion into computer networks.

---

[179] NSA. NSA's Top Ten Cybersecurity Mitigation Strategies. *National Security Agency*. https://www.nsa.gov/Portals/70/documents/what-we-do/cybersecurity/professional-resources/csi-nsas-top10-cybersecurity-mitigation-strategies.pdf

[180] James MacMullen. An Introduction to Advanced Persistent Threat (APT) Campaigns. *TechGenix*. 22 November 2022. What Are Advanced Persistent Threat (APT) Campaigns? (techgenix.com)

THOUGHTS ON PRIVACY

"All human beings have three lives: public, private, and secret."
Gabriel García Márquez

"Eventually all things are known. And few matter."
Gore Vidal

"People don't value their obscurity. They don't know what it's like to have it taken away..."
Bob Dylan

"We are rapidly entering the age of no privacy, where everyone is open to surveillance at all times; where there are no secrets from government."
William O. Douglas

"Friends don't spy; true friendship is about privacy, too."
Stephen King

Top Intelligent Operations (AI Products) in 2023

Private sector investment in AI technology – denominated as *intelligence operations* (IO) - continue to expand, but the pace of investment is subject to economic trends, just like investments in capital goods. When the economy is expanding, investments in new technology increase, and when the economy is contracting, so do investments. A contracting economy suffering from inflation at the start of 2023 is not the best climate to invest in new technology. Nevertheless, everyone wants to make faster and smarter decisions, and AI is regarded as a smart way to introduce innovation and achieve intelligent success. In January 2017, R. L. Adams in an article published in *Forbes*, predicted that together with quantum computers, '*AI will continue to expand to address complex problems, including aging, disease, war, poverty, famine, the origins of the universe and deep space exploration.*'[181] The same prediction could be re-issued in January 2023. Amelia Scott predicted that in 2023 that new and more advanced versions of AI-driven software will be introduced. Including advances in text-to-image AI platforms, improved Machine Learning engineering, and advances in robotics technology.[182]

Among the key areas of interest to introduce and expand AI in 2023, are automated financial investing, banking, budgeting, financial operations, business services, cash-flow forecasting, healthcare management, human resources and talent search, marketing, national security-defense operations, predictive analytics, productivity, robotics, supply chain, sourcing and procurement, scenario analysis, self-driving cars, smart assistant, social media monitoring, virtual travel booking agent, and other areas in which AI is operating in the background.

As AI technology advances, cybercriminals will try to incorporate it into their criminal enterprises, including disinformation, deepfakes, phishing, and all kinds of scam tactics. AI technology will be used to expand security procedures to detect all kinds of maligned actors and neutralize their operations. Without a doubt, there will an expansion in the constant tug-of-war between good the evil.[183]

---

[181] R.L. Adams. 10 Powerful Examples of Artificial Intelligence In Use Today. *Forbes*. 10 January 2023. 10 Powerful Examples Of Artificial Intelligence In Use Today (forbes.com)

[182] Amelia Scott. Artificial Intelligence Predictions in 2023. The-next-tech.com. Artificial Intelligence Predictions In 2023 | The Next Tech (the-next-tech.com)

[183] Stephen Weigand. 2023 tech predictions: AI and machine learning will come into their own for security. SCmagazine.com 30 December 2022. 2023 tech predictions: AI and machine learning will come into their own for security | SC Media (scmagazine.com)

POPULAR AI PRODUCTS IN 2023 – SAMPLE

PRODUCTS	DESCRIPTION[184] [185]
Alexa	AI-powered voice assistant, produced by Amazon, to power its website and assist with all the company activities, including warehouse robots that grab, sort, and ship products to customers.
AlphaSense	An AI-powered financial search engine that can analyze multiple data points for investment firms.
Botminds	AI for vertical integration, and end-to-end automation, including automated invoice processing, risk management, access, verification, and validation risks.
Collective [i]	AI for sales forecasting and benchmarks, revenue projections based on historical trends, business trends, cash flow, predicting revenue, performance benchmarking, competitor product innovations, qualitative and quantitative sales forecasting, and opinion forecasting.
Cortana	Microsoft's smart assistant for *Windows Phone 8.1* and integrated into the *Microsoft 365* suite of apps.
Cresta	AI Real-time agent assistance and coaching.
Forethought	AI platform for customer support automation.
Hanson Robotics	AI-operated humanoid robots for the commercial and consumer markets. For example, *Sophia*, one of the humanoid robots, is a social-learning robot.
Predict	AI to analyze behavioral data, improve user engagement, drive in-store and online sales, and boost brand awareness.
iRobot	Introduced *Roomba*, a smart, robotic vacuum cleaner using AI to vacuum clean a room, identifying obstacles, room size, and other factors to clean floors.
Self-driving cars	AI to operate self-driving cars using multiple sensors collecting thousands of data points every millisecond. Several companies are investing in this technology, including Google, Tesla, Luminar, and multiple vehicle manufacturers.
Siri	Apple's digital assistant is integrated into the iPhone.
Socure	AI to verify identity and fraud prediction, and predict risk, for financial institutions, banks, online gaming, healthcare insurance, and other businesses.
Softbank Robotics	AI-driven humanoid robot known as *Pepper*, using biometrics, can recognize people and human emotions, and can communicate using multiple languages. Other products include an autonomous vacuum cleaner named *Whiz*.
Splunk Enterprise	AI is used to search, collect, analyze, visualize, and index data in a multi-cloud and hybrid environment.
Virtual VetNurse	AI-supported integrated digital platform for busy veterinary clinics, promote products and services, arrange post-surgery follow-up, telemedicine, online pet care, bookings, online '*puppy school*' and other training, and online pet care topics.
WebHR	AI tool to handle human resources from 'hire' to 'retire.'
Well	Using AI, this product provides personalized medical guidance, including vaccination advice, specific condition guidance, and recommend doctors visits

---

[184] Sam Daley. 31 Examples of Artificial Intelligence Shaking Up Business as Usual. *Builtin*.com.18 August 2022. 31 Top Artificial Intelligence Examples You Should Know 2023 | Built In

[185] Elisha Odemakinde. The 13 Most Popular AI Software Products in 2023. *Viso.ai*. The 13 Most Popular AI Software Products in 2023 - viso.ai

Ransomware Cybercriminals

The term *"ransomware"* is the equivalent of *'extortion'* by cybercriminals in the age of IT and AI. It is defined as *'a way to enter a victim's computers and databanks to encrypt the victim's files and demand payment of a ransom to recover the files.'* The costs associated with this criminal activity can be very high, and cause serious disruptions to the public and private sectors. Criminal elements will always try to find ways to violate cyber security, including ways to weaponize and harness AI, to exploit exposed data.

There are multiple methods used by these cybercriminals, but *'phishing'* is prevalent. They send emails to potential victims claiming to be from reputable companies to reach vulnerable individuals to induce (scam) them to reveal personal or company information, such as passwords, or download an attachment. Social engineering is frequently used to confuse victims. Through the use of AI, potential victims can defend against scammers using advanced security systems to deal with the threat by blocking malware. AI can be used to identify unusual behavior and anomalies associated with fraud. Through AI, the defensive systems are updated daily as the scammers change tactics.[186] [187]

In 2022 alone, there were numerous victims. The normal practice is to use *'phishing'* and related social engineering practices to confuse a victim and gain entry to computer systems. In the U.S. alone, it is estimated that about 200 public sector entities, including at least 105 local governments, 44 universities, 45 school districts, and about 290 hospitals were targeted by ransomware attacks.

---

[186] Brad. AI In Phishing: How Artificial Intelligence Can Act as Both, A boon and Bane When it Comes to Phishing. *PhishingProtection.com*. 15 July 2021. AI In Phishing: How Artificial Intelligence Can Act as Both, A Boon and Bane When It Comes to Phishing | PhishProtection.com

[187] Sennovate. The role of artificial intelligence in detecting phishing attacks. *Sennovate*. 3 January 2023. How to detect Phishing attacks with Artificial Intelligence (sennovate.com)

Top Ransomware Gangs

Among the leading criminal gangs associated with ransomware attacks are:[188] [189] [190] [191] [192]

- **Black Cat (BlackMatter):** Among the victims of these cyber criminals based in Eastern Europe was the Austrian State of Carinthia. The attack disrupted the delivery of government services to the community. The government refused to pay, and the attackers expanded their penetration of more government entities, including hacking internal email services. The same cybercriminals attacked Wheat Ridge, part of the Denver, Colorado municipal services. The same group targeted the University of Pisa in Italy, again making ransom payment demands to release the hacked data. The Cybersecurity and Infrastructure Security Agency (CISA) and the FBI issued a warning about these cybercriminals on 18 October 2021. In a FLASH alert published in April 2022, the FBI revealed that the operation had infected more than 60 victims since first surfacing in mid-November 2021.[193] [194]

- **Conti:** These cybercriminals targeted among other victims several branches of the Government of Costa Rica, and demanded $20 million in ransom. The Cybersecurity and Infrastructure Security Agency (CISA) and the FBI have observed the increased use of Conti ransomware in more than 400 attacks on U.S. and international organizations. In typical Conti

---

[188] Anthony Webb. 2022 Ransomware Attacks and Evolution of Data Exfiltration. *CXOToday.com*. 28 December 2022. 2022 Ransomware Attacks and Evolution of Data Exfiltration (cxotoday.com)

[189] Miklos Zoltan. 16 Biggest Ransomware Attacks in 2022. *Privacy Affairs*. October 2022. 16 Biggest Ransomware Attacks in 2022 - Privacy Affairs

[190] Cyber Management. 5 Major Ransomware Attacks of 2022. *Cyber Management*. 15 June 2022. 5 Major Ransomware Attacks of 2022 (cm-alliance.com)

[191] SC Staff. US Hit with deluge of ransomware attacks in 2022. SC Media. 3 January 2023. US hit with deluge of ransomware attacks in 2022 | SC Media (scmagazine.com)

[192] Pierluigi Paganini. Ransomeware attacks hit 105 US local governments in 2022. *Securityaffairs.com*. 3 January 2023. Ransomware attacks hit 105 US local governments in 2022Security Affairs

[193] U.S. Government. CISA, FBI, and NSA Release BlackMatter ransomeware advisory to help organizations reduce risk of attack. Cybersecurity & Infrastructure Agency. 18 October 2021.

[194] U.S. Government. Breaking Down the BlackCat Ransomware Operations. Cybersecurity & Infrastructure Agency. Breaking Down the BlackCat Ransomware Operation (cisecurity.org)

ransomware attacks, malicious cyber actors steal files, encrypt servers and workstations, and demand a ransom payment. These criminals use spearphishing emails with malicious attachments, stolen or weak Remote Desktop Protocols, fake software, and exploit other vulnerabilities.[195]

- **CUBA**: A cybercriminal gang that uses the name Cuba was very active in 2022, continuing operations since first surfacing in 2019, according to the FBI and CISA. It uses the appendix '. *cuba'* extension when it encrypts files of victims. Usual targets are public institutions, financial, healthcare, food brokers, and IT companies. Among the usual tools they use are RomCom RAT, KerberCache, ZeroLogon, and similar tools. Based on published reports, this is a Russian criminal organization. *"Third-party and open-source reports have identified a possible link between Cuba ransomware actors, RomCom Remote Access Trojan (RAT) actors, and Industrial Spy ransomware actors."* It is estimated by the FBI and CISA that this criminal gang earned over $60 million in 2022 from their criminal enterprise. [196] [197] [198]

- **Dridex:** This is malware used to target banks that use Apple's macOS operating system using Novel Infection Method. Because actors using Dridex malware and its derivatives continue to target the financial services sector, including financial institutions and customers, CISA issued a report about the techniques, tactics, and procedures used by Dridex, which was assessed to be a Russia-Based cybercriminal organization. They were assessed to use the so-called *"Bugat"* malware. According to the report: *"Phishing messages employ a combination of legitimate business names and domains, professional terminology, and language implying urgency to persuade victims to activate open attachments. Sender e-mail addresses can simulate individuals (name@domain.com), administrative (admin@domain.com, support@domain.com), or common "do not reply" local parts (noreply@domain.com). Subject and attachment titles can include*

---

[195] U.S. Government. Alert (AA21-265A) Conti Ransomware. *Cybersecurity & Infrastructure Agency*. 9 March 2022. Conti Ransomware | CISA

[196] Ionut Archire. Over 100 Organizations Hit by Cuba Ransomware: CISA, FBI. *Security Week*. 2 December 2022. Over 100 Organizations Hit by Cuba Ransomware: CISA, FBI | SecurityWeek.Com

[197] U.S. Government. #StopRansomware: Cuba Ransomware. *National Cyber Awareness System*. 1 December 2022. #StopRansomware: Cuba Ransomware | CISA

[198] Sumeet Wadhwani. CISA and FBI Say Cuba Ransomware's Lifetime Earnings Crossed $60M in 2022. *Spiceworks*. 5 December 2022. CISA and FBI Say Cuba Ransomware's Lifetime Earnings Crossed $60M in 2022 | Spiceworks

typical terms such as "invoice", "order", "scan", "receipt", "debit note", "itinerary", and others." [199] [200]

- **Lapsus$:** These hackers stole a huge amount of data from the largest semiconductor company Nvidia, which elected to pay an estimated $1 million in ransom. They stole an estimated 1 TB of information. However, the victim, in this case, carried out a counterattack hack against the cybercriminals. The criminals then carried out their counterattack, leaking Nvidia data. This particular set of cybercriminals is thought to be operating in a South American country.[201]

- **LockBit (formerly known as ABCD):** This ransomware was used to attack several hospitals in France, including the *Centre Hospitalier Sud Francilien* and the *André Mignot Hospital.* These attacks consisted of the exfiltration of data, including patient information, and serious disruptions to the operation of the hospitals. The facilities had to be closed temporarily and patients had to be moved to other hospitals. These particular bandits demand financial payments normally in Bitcoin payments for the decryption of the stolen data. If the victims do not pay the demanded ransom, the stolen data is rendered permanently inaccessible. These cybercriminals walked away with at least $10 million. They also carried out a cyberattack against a chain of healthcare services in Argentina called OSDE. The criminal gang demanded a ransom of about $300,000, threatening to erase all the hacked files. The FBI issued a Flash report on LockBit 2.0 on 7 February 2022.[202]

- **REvil:** This particular gang searches for vulnerable entities who want to avoid publicity if their files are hacked. A usual tactic is to use phishing attacks to gain entry into computer systems. The FBI, U.S. Cyber Command, and the Secret Service together with other countries for the second time hacked and forced offline this cybercriminal enterprise in 2021. These cybercriminals seem to be resilient, and able to restart criminal activities, despite being targeted by law enforcement. This

---

[199] The Hacker News. Dridex Malware Now Attacking macOS Systems with Novel Infection Method. *The Hacker News.* 6 January 2023. Thehackernews.com/2023/01/Dridex-malware-biw-attacking-macos.html

[200] U.S. Government. Alert (AA19-339A) Dridex Malware. Cybersecurity & Infrastructure Agency.5 December 2019. Dridex Malware | CISA

[201] Sumeet Wadhwani. Ransomware Group Lapsus$ Cries Foul After NVIDIA Allegedly Does a Tit-for-Tat. *Spiceworks.* 4 March 2022. Ransomware Group Lapsus$ Cries Foul After NVIDIA Allegedly Does a Tit-for-Tat | Spiceworks

[202] U.S. Government. FBI Releases Indicators of Compromise Associated with LockBit 2.0 *Ransomware.* FBI. 7 February 2022. FBI Releases Indicators of Compromise Associated with LockBit 2.0 Ransomware | CISA

particular organization seems to be a Russian cybercriminal group. Another name used to refer to this organization is Evil Corp.[203]

- **SpyNote:** Targets financial institutions using Android malware, for the most part in Europe. This gang produces malware and sells it to other hacking organizations. Among the victims are: Deutsche Bank, HSBC, Kotak Mahindra Bank, Nubank, and Kotak. Among other things, this hacking organization siphons banking credentials.[204]

There are several other active cybercriminal gangs, but they tend to change names and tactics as they gain more experience. Among them are Black Basta, CMCC, CryWiper, DopplePaymer, Endurance, FIN7, Maze, Mindware, Raas, and Raspberry Robin. To what extent these criminal gangs use AI is a difficult question to answer. Without a doubt, some of them have backing from a national government and are part of an intelligence organization.

CISA, FBI, NSA, the Australian Cyber Security Centre (ACSC), and the UL's National Cyber Security Center (NCSC-UK), together with other allies are working together to deal with the increasing global threat of cybercriminals using ransomware.[205] On 26 January 2023, the FBI reported that it had disrupted the operations of the prominent ransomware gang called Hive. U.S. Justice Department hackers broke into the gang's network and put it under surveillance to alert potential future victims of a ransomware attack. The action was coordinated with law enforcement authorities in Germany and the Netherlands. Over the years, Hive was able to collect over $100 million in ransomware from at least 1500 victims.[206]

---

[203] Maggie Miller. US, allied nations force REvil ransomware group offline: report. *The Hill.* 21 October 2021. US, allied nations force REvil ransomware group offline: report | The Hill

[204] The Hacker News. SpyNote Strikes Again: Android Spyware Targeting Financial Institutions. *The Hacker News.* 5 January 2023. Thehackernews.com/2023/01/spynote-strikes-again-android-spyware.html

[205] Press Release. CISA, FBI, NSA, and International Partners Issue Advisory on Ransomware Trends from 2021. NSA/CSS. 9 February 2022. CISA, FBI, NSA and International Partners Issue Advisory on Ransomware Trends from 2021 > National Security Agency/Central Security Service > Article

[206] Sarah N. Lynch and Raphael Satter. U.S. says it 'hacked the hackers' to bring down ransomware gang, helping 300 victims. Reuters. 26 January 2023. U.S. says it 'hacked the hackers' to bring down ransomware gang, helping 300 victims (yahoo.com)

Convicted Russian Cyber Criminals

Roman Valeryevich Seleznev, aka *Track2*, A 32-year-old Vladivostok, Russian, was sentenced today to 27 years in prison for his computer hacking crimes that caused more than $169 million in damage to small businesses and financial institutions. He was convicted in August 2016, of 38 counts related to his scheme to hack into point-of-sale computers to steal credit card numbers and sell them on dark market websites District Judge Richard A. Jones of the Western District of Washington imposed the sentence.[207]

Note: Seleznev is the son of a Russian Member of Parliament. (Federal Assembly or *'Duma'*)

Aleksandr Zhukov, a Russian-born British businessman, who was arrested in Bulgaria in 2018, was extradited to the United States in 2019 and was sentenced by United States District Judge Eric R. Komitee to 10 years imprisonment for perpetrating a digital advertising fraud scheme through which the defendant and his co-conspirators stole more than $7 million from U.S. advertisers, publishers, platforms, and others in the U.S. digital advertising industry. Zhukov was convicted following a jury trial in May 2021 of wire fraud conspiracy, wire fraud, money laundering conspiracy, and money laundering. To create the illusion that human internet users were viewing the advertisements loaded onto these spoofed webpages, Zhukov and his co-conspirators programmed the bots to appear and behave like human internet users: falsely representing that they had screens and mouses, that they were running operating systems used for personal computers, and that they were running commercially available internet browsers (like Chrome, Internet Explorer, and Firefox) when they were not.[208]

NOTE: Australia, Canada, New Zealand, the U.K., and the U.S. released a Joint Cybersecurity Advisory on 20 April 2022, stating that Russian state-sponsored cyber actors and Russian-aligned cybercriminals could increase their malicious activities in light of the invasion of Ukraine in 2022.[209]

Vladislav Klyushin, a Russian cybercriminal was convicted in Massachusetts on 14 February 2023, of participating in an elaborate insider trading scheme using data hacked from U.S. computer networks. He was arrested in Switzerland in 2021.[210] This individual and his company have a long history of cooperating with the Kremlin, particularly with Russian intelligence organizations. He is a former member of the GRU. Russia has harbored hackers like this criminal for years. This is not an unusual case.

---

[207] U.S. Department of Justice. Russian Cyber-Criminal Sentenced to 27 Years in Prison for Hacking and Credit Card Fraud Scheme. *U.S. Department of Justice.* 21 April 2017.

[208] U.S. Attorney for the Eastern District of New York. Russian Cybercriminal Sentenced to 10 Years in Prison for Digital Advertising Fraud Scheme. *U.S. Department of Justice.* 10 November 2021.

[209] National Cyber Awareness System. Russian State-Sponsored and Criminal Cyber Threats to Critical Infrastructure. U.S. National Cyber Awareness System. 20 April 2022. Russian State-Sponsored and Criminal Cyber Threats to Critical Infrastructure | CISA

[210] Alanna Durkin Richer. Russian businessman guilty in hacking insider trade scheme. AP News. 13 February 2023. Russian businessman guilty in hacking, insider trade scheme | AP News

Russian Cybercriminals Wanted by the FBI

These "wanted" FBI posters represent a sample of the known cybercriminals operating from Russia, targeting private and government institutions globally. Most of them have links to Russian intelligence, including the Federal Security Service (FSB), Foreign Intelligence Service (SVR), the Federal Protective Service (FSO), and the Main Intelligence Directorate (military intelligence) (GRU), successor to the Soviet KGB, and sister intelligence organizations.

RUSSIAN FSB CENTER 16 HACKERS

Conspiracy to Commit Computer Intrusions; Conspiracy to Commit Wire Fraud; Wire Fraud; Computer Fraud – Unauthorized Access to Obtain Information from Protected Computers; Aggravated Identity Theft; Aiding and Abetting

PAVEL ALEKSANDROVICH AKULOV
(Павел Александрович Акулов)

MIKHAIL MIKHAILOVICH GAVRILOV
(Михаил Михайлович Гаврилов)

MARAT VALERYEVICH TYUKOV
(Марат Валерьевич Тюков)

WANTED BY THE FBI

ALEXSEY BELAN

Computer Intrusion; Aggravated Identity Theft; Fraud in Connection With a Computer

DESCRIPTION

Aliases: Aleksei Belan, Aleksey Belan, Alekkey Aleksayevich Belan, Alexsey Alexseyevich Belan, Alexsei Belan, Abyr Valgov, "Abyrvalg", "Fedyunya", "Magg", "M4G", "Moy Yaszik"

Date(s) of Birth Used: June 27, 1987
Place of Birth: Riga, Latvia
Hair: Brown
Eyes: Blue
Height: 6'0"
Weight: 175 pounds
Sex: Male
Race: White
Occupation: Computer/Network Engineer and Software Programmer
Nationality: Latvian
NCIC: W507648159

REWARD

The FBI is offering a reward of up to $100,000 for information leading to the arrest of Alexsey Belan.

REMARKS

Belan has Russian citizenship and is known to hold a Russian passport. He speaks Russian and may travel to Russia, Greece, Latvia, the Maldives, and Thailand. He may wear eyeglasses and dye his brown hair red or blond. He was last known to be in Athens, Greece.

CAUTION

Between January of 2012, and April of 2013, Alexsey Belan is alleged to have intruded the computer networks of three major United States-based e-commerce companies in Nevada and California. He is alleged to have stolen their user databases which he then exported and made readily accessible on his server. Belan allegedly stole the user data and the encrypted passwords of millions of accounts and then negotiated the sales of the databases.

Two separate federal arrest warrants for Belan have been issued. One was issued on September 12, 2012, in the United States District Court, District of Nevada, Las Vegas, Nevada, after Belan was charged with obtaining information by computer from a protected computer, possession of fifteen or more unauthorized access devices, and aggravated identity theft. The second warrant was issued on June 6, 2013, in the United States District Court, Northern District of California, San Francisco, California, after Belan was charged with two counts of fraud in connection with a computer and two counts of aggravated identity theft.

SHOULD BE CONSIDERED AN INTERNATIONAL FLIGHT RISK

If you have any information concerning this person, please contact your local FBI office or the nearest American Embassy or Consulate.

Field Offices: Las Vegas, San Francisco

IGOR ANATOLYEVICH SUSHCHIN

Conspiring to Commit Computer Fraud and Abuse; Accessing a Computer Without Authorization for the Purpose of Commercial Advantage and Private Financial Gain; Damaging a Computer Through the Transmission of Code and Commands; Economic Espionage; Theft of Trade Secrets; Access Device Fraud; Wire Fraud

DESCRIPTION

Aliases: Igor Suchin, Igor Sutchin
Date(s) of Birth Used: August 28, 1971
Hair: Blond
Sex: Male
Nationality: Russian

Place of Birth: Moscow, Russia
Eyes: Blue
Race: White

REMARKS

Sushchin has Russian citizenship and is known to hold a Russian passport. Sushchin is alleged to be a Russian Federal Security Service (FSB) Officer of unknown rank. In addition to working for the FSB, he is alleged to have served as Head of Information Security for a Russian company, providing information about employees of that company to the FSB. He was last known to be in Moscow, Russia.

CAUTION

From at least January of 2014, continuing through December of 2016, Igor Anatolyevich Sushchin is alleged to have conspired with, among others, known and unknown FSB officers, including Dmitry Aleksandrovich Dokuchaev, to protect, direct, facilitate, and pay criminal hackers, including Alexsey Belan. Sushchin and his conspirators agreed to, and did, gain unauthorized access to the computer networks of and user accounts hosted at major companies providing worldwide webmail and internet related services in the Northern District of California and elsewhere.

A federal arrest warrant for Igor Anatolyevich Sushchin was issued on February 28, 2017, in the United States District Court, Northern District of California, San Francisco, California. That warrant was based on an indictment charging him with conspiring to commit computer fraud and abuse; accessing a computer without authorization for the purpose of commercial advantage and private financial gain; damaging a computer through the transmission of code and commands; economic espionage; theft of trade secrets; access device fraud; and wire fraud.

SHOULD BE CONSIDERED AN INTERNATIONAL FLIGHT RISK

If you have any information concerning this person, please contact your local FBI office or the nearest American Embassy or Consulate.

WANTED BY THE FBI

Conspiracy to Commit Wire Fraud; Conspiracy to Commit Computer-Related Fraud (Computer Intrusion); Wire Fraud; Computer Intrusion

ANDREY NABILEVICH TAAME

Multimedia: Images

Aliases:
Andrei Taame, Andri Taame, Andrey Taame

DESCRIPTION

Date(s) of Birth Used:	March 19, 1980	Hair:	Brown
Place of Birth:	Damascus, Syria	Eyes:	Brown
Height:	5'10"	Sex:	Male
Weight:	165 pounds	Race:	White
NCIC:	W213929230		

Remarks: Taame speaks both English and Russian. He holds a Russian passport and Russian citizenship. He may have travelled to Cyprus or Russia.

WANTED
BY THE FBI

Conspiracy to Participate in Racketeering Activity; Bank Fraud; Conspiracy to Violate the Computer Fraud and Abuse Act; Conspiracy to Violate the Identity Theft and Assumption Deterrence Act; Aggravated Identity Theft; Conspiracy; Computer Fraud; Wire Fraud; Money Laundering; Conspiracy to Commit Bank Fraud

EVGENIY MIKHAILOVICH BOGACHEV

Multimedia: Images

Aliases:
Yevgeniy Bogachev, Evgeniy Mikhaylovich Bogachev, "lucky12345", "slavik", "Pollingsoon"

Date(s) of Birth Used: October 28, 1983

Hair: Brown (usually shaves his head)

WANTED BY THE FBI

CONSPIRACY TO COMMIT COMPUTER FRAUD; CONSPIRACY TO COMMIT WIRE FRAUD; WIRE FRAUD; AGGRAVATED IDENTITY THEFT; CONSPIRACY TO COMMIT MONEY LAUNDERING

GRU HACKING TO UNDERMINE ANTI-DOPING EFFORTS

Dmitriy Sergeyevich Badin | Artem Andreyevich Malyshev | Alexey Valerevich Minin | Aleksei Sergeyevich Morenets

Evgenii Mikhaylovich Serebriakov | Oleg Mikhaylovich Sotnikov | Ivan Sergeyevich Yermakov

DETAILS

On October 3, 2018, a federal grand jury sitting in the Western District of Pennsylvania returned an indictment against 7 Russian individuals for their alleged roles in hacking and related influence and disinformation operations targeting, among others, international anti-doping agencies, sporting federations, and anti-doping officials. The indictment charges Dmitriy Sergeyevich Badin, Artem Andreyevich Malyshev, Alexey Valerevich Minin, Aleksei Sergeyevich Morenets, Evgenii Mikhaylovich Serebriakov, Oleg Mikhaylovich Sotnikov, and Ivan Sergeyevich Yermakov, with computer hacking activity spanning from 2014 through May of 2018, including the computer intrusions of the United States Anti-Doping Agency (USADA), the World Anti-Doping Agency (WADA), and other victim entities during the 2016 Summer Olympics and Paralympics and afterwards. The indictment charges these defendants with conspiracy to commit computer fraud, conspiracy to commit wire fraud, wire fraud, aggravated identity theft, and conspiracy to commit money laundering. The United States District Court for the Western District of Pennsylvania in Pittsburgh, Pennsylvania, issued a federal arrest warrant for each of these defendants upon the grand jury's return of the indictment.

THESE INDIVIDUALS SHOULD BE CONSIDERED ARMED AND DANGEROUS, AN INTERNATIONAL FLIGHT RISK, AND AN ESCAPE RISK

If you have any information concerning this case, please contact your local FBI office, or the nearest American Embassy or Consulate.

www.fbi.gov

Online Content Generated by AI by 2025

> Times and conditions change so rapidly that we must keep our aim constantly focused on the future.
>
> **Walt Disney**

It has been predicted that by 2025, an estimated 90% of all online content could be generated by AI. According to Alexandra Garfinkle, a Senior Reporter for Yahoo Finance, generative Ai, could completely revamp practically all digital online content. One of the applications, ChatGPT, as well as other competing applications, are already working on so-called generative AI. Audio, pictures, video, and other content on the web may be produced by multiple apps using AI. Companies like Microsoft and Google are already working at an accelerated rate on the subject.[211] In other words, Generative AI consists of unsupervised machine learning technology that can discover, collect, process, and based on patterns and trends, produce new 'things' without human interaction.

But what is *Generative AI*? It consists of AI algorithms that use existing content to create new content, by allowing computers to identify and abstract input patterns, to generate similar content without human participation using machine learning. In the future, robots will be able to understand abstract concepts. For example, through the use of AI, old films could be restored and enhanced, improving sound, color, and sharpness. This technology is not necessarily all good. Malicious actors could use the technology to scam people with fake news and other fraudulent actions. Among other capabilities, through Generative AI, fake human faces, objects, and scenes can be generated to look like real pictures. Without a doubt, this technology will have a mix of advantages and disadvantages, like so many other areas of AI.[212] [213] [214]

---

[211] Alexandra Garfinkle. 90% of online content could be 'generated by AI by 2025,' experts say. Yahoo Finance. 13 January 2023. 90% of online content could be 'generated by AI by 2025,' expert says (yahoo.com)

[212] Market Trends. What is Generative AI, Its Impacts and Limitations? *Analytics Insight*. 16 January 2021. What is Generative AI, Its Impacts and Limitations? (analyticsinsight.net)

[213] Hazal Simsek. A Complete Guide to Generative AI in 2023. *AI Multiple*. 26 December 2022. A Complete Guide to Generative AI in 2023 (aimultiple.com)

[214] Generative AI: All You Need to Know. Murf Resources. 6 January 2023. Generative AI : All you need to know | Murf AI

Autonomous Vehicles and Passenger Planes

The advent of driverless vehicles has been in the headlines for some time, but every company that has tried to introduce them into the market, including Tesla, has run into serious challenges. As if that was not challenging enough for AI, now fully autonomous passenger planes are being designed using AI technology. Leading aerospace companies, including Boeing and Airbus, are engaged in their development. The emphasis has reportedly been placed on automatic landing systems to assist a human pilot in bad weather landings. Multiple companies are working closely with the Federal Aviation Administration (FAA) and NASA to advance the development of AI-driven autonomous aircraft. Although planes flying without a pilot may be far into the future, the technology's first target may be to allow commercial planes using AI technology to be allowed to fly with only one human pilot, instead of the currently required two.[215]

The Air Line Pilots Association, and taxi and rideshare drivers may have found common ground to oppose the development of technology that constitute a risk to their livelihoods. How these sectors will convince the traveling public to place their safety in robots may be more challenging than developing AI algorithms for self-driving and autonomous flights.

Humanoids, *Gynoids,* and *Fembots*

Among the multiple efforts in motion related to AI, are the efforts to create *'humanoid'* robots, modeled after the human body, with legs, arms, hands, etc. One of the stated goals is to address the so-called *'labor shortage,'* with robots that can do work that humans do not want to do for one reason or another. AI-powered machine tools make sense, and thousands have been operating in factories for a very long time. Humanoid robots or *'robonauts,'* are entirely different things, possibly due to a fixation on looks, then on performance capabilities. Multiple prototypes of humanoid robots exist already, but they seem to be more focused on *'show'* than actual performance. Aesthetics or skills? It is difficult to figure out what the aims are, as they overlap. Is the intention to create a thinking humanoid that functions fully as a human, or something way short of that goal?[216]

---

[215] Alex Fitzpatrick. Fully autonomous passenger planes are inching closer to takeoff. *AXIOS*. 3 February 2023. Fully autonomous passenger planes are inching closer to takeoff (axios.com)

[216] The race to build AI-powered humanoids is heating up. DNYUZ. 2 March 2023. The race to build AI-powered humanoids is heating up – DNyuz

Humanoid robots could conceivably perform tasks similar to those performed by humans if driven by AI with algorithms written for that purpose. Conceivably, they could collect garbage, and support military operations by replacing human operators of airplanes, tanks, and other equipment. They could work as cashiers and guards, or entertain people. However, all of these tasks can be performed by machines that do not necessarily look like a human. Like anything else, they may have advantages and disadvantages. But what does that have to do with an anthropomorphic design? Is the goal to create machines that can show anger, joy, sadness, and a full range of human emotions?[217]

Humanoid robots of a 'female variety' are referred to as *'gynoids'* and *'fembots.'* Assigning gender to a robot in the *Woke* culture could be extremely controversial. What is the point of assigning a gender to a robot? Are they supposed to be life-size love dolls? What is the difference between a silicone doll and a gynoid? Ultrarealistic silicone dolls are already on the market, but they have nothing to do with the concept of a humanoid robot, or do they? Science fiction comes alive with AI!

Sample of companies working on Humanoid Robots

Agility Robotics (USA)	**Macco Robotics (Spain)**
Boston Dynamics (USA)	**PAL Robotics (Spain)**
Canonical Group (UK)	**PSYGIG, Inc. (Japan)**
Computer Science (USA)	**QBMT (Belgium)**
Devanthrop (Germany)	**React AI (Aiseedo) (UK)**
Dyson (UK)	**Robotis (South Korea)**
Google (Alphabet Inc.) (USA)	**Samsung Electronics**
Honda Motors (Japan)	**Sastra Robotics (India)**
Hoomano (France)	**Shadow Robot Company (UK)**
Intuitive Robots (France)	**Tesla (Optimus robot)**
Jinn-Bot Robotics (Switzerland)	**Toyota Motor (Japan)**
Kindred Systems (USA)	**Ubtech (PRC-China)**
Leju (PRC – China)	

---

[217] Heba Soffar. Humanoid robots uses, types, risks, advantages and disadvantages. *Science Online*. 5 February 2023. Humanoid robots uses, types, risks, advantages and disadvantages | Science online (online-sciences.com)

Predictive Analytics Generated by AI

A *'prediction,'* is a statement about what someone thinks will happen in the future, based on experience, prior observations, patterns based on prior events, or data analysis. The extraction of information from raw data to be used to predict future trends and behavioral patterns is referred to as *'predictive analytics.'* [218] [219] It is a form of *"regression analysis,"* or a statistical process for estimating the relationships among variables. It is a form of *'predictive modeling,'* to forecast or anticipate the *'probability'* of an outcome using modeling methods that include, AI, machine learning, and statistics.[220]

- *Predictive Analytics* uses *'mathematical modeling'* tools to generate predictions:
    - About a future event,
    - About an unknown fact,
    - About any type of unknown scenario in the future.

- *Predictive Analytics* uses *'linear regression'* modeling tools to predict an unknown based on a predetermined set of quantifiable data.

- *Predictive Analytics* can use text mining tools to comb databases, and generate predictions as to the "most likely' outcomes based on prior experience reflected in databases.

AI tools (algorithms) capture relationships among multiple *'data points'* and *'factors'* to assess the *'potential outcomes* associated with a particular set of conditions. However, the *'predictions'* are not always accurate.

If the data points contain false information, the analytical process is bound to fail. *'Garbage in, garbage out.'* Social media, for example, can feed good and false information and nonsense. Social media is vulnerable to misinformation. Predictive analytical algorithms are hostage to data quality. Nevertheless, it is being used for planning and to simulate potential scenarios to obtain better outcomes in multiple areas, such as cyber security, energy, financial planning, healthcare, insurance, marketing, supply chain management, weather forecasting, fundraising, workforce planning, sports, law enforcement, and

---

[218] Clay Halton. Predictive Analytics. *Investopedia.* 30 June 2021. https://www.investopedia.com/terms/p/predictive-analytics.asp

[219] Jacqueline Biscobing. Definition: Predictive analytics. *TechTarget.* https://searchbusinessanalytics.techtarget.com/definition/predictive-analytics

[220] Ashley DiFranza. Predictive Analytics: What It Is & Why it's Important. *Northeastern.edu.* 17 February 2021. Predictive Analytics: What It Is & Why It's Important (northeastern.edu)

national security. Predictive analytics for law enforcement and national security is widely used by multiple countries.²²¹

'Predictions' are statements of what will happen in the future, and 'prophecies' are predictions with some religious connotations made by an alleged "*wise*" person or '*prophet*' in some sacred text. The *Oxford Dictionary* defines "*prediction*" as *an act of saying or estimating that (a specified thing) will happen in the future or will be a consequence of something.* ²²² Fortune-tellers and soothsayers have been around making predictions for hundreds of years. Some allegedly used '*crystal balls*' as some form of pseudoscience. In the 8th century BC, there was a soothsayer and priestess named Pythia in Ancient Greece, known as the '*Oracle of Delphi*,' who practice 'divination' in the theater or '*Temple of Apollo.*' *Pythia* was considered the mouthpiece of Apollo, the God of Revelation. The ruins of these famous sites at located on Mount Parnassus, about 75 miles from Athens.²²³ Another famous '*seer*' was Michel de Nostradamus (1503-1566), a French astrologer, physician, apothecary, and author of the 1555 book *Les Prophéties*, with a collection of over 900 predictions. More recently, in the U.S., we had Jean Dixon, who claimed to be an '*astrologist*,' who provided advice to Presidents Franklin D. Roosevelt and Richard Nixon. The difference between these historical figures to do mainly with religious connotations. Emotional intelligence? Are AI and religion compatible? AI is no longer imaginary, it is a reality, and a part of everyday life. ²²⁴ As previously mentioned, ethics and morals, are not part of AI systems.

Library of Congress Collection
Oracle of Delphi / Temple to Apollo In Greece

---

²²¹ Will Carless. Feds are tracking American's social media to identify dangerous conspiracies. Critics worry for civil liberties. *USA Today*. 14 May 2021.
https://www.usatoday.com/story/news/nation/2021/05/14/terrorist-social-media-narratives-focus-new-dhs-effort/5075237001/

²²² According to the Catholic Church… *in speaking about end-times prophecy, the Bible warns us to adhere to Sacred Tradition and Sacred Scripture. Saint Peter states unequivocally that "no prophecy of Scripture is a matter of one's own interpretation" (2 Peter 1:20); therefore, prophecy is a matter of public interpretation in the Church, "the pillar and bulwark of the truth" (1 Timothy 3:15).*

²²³ Pythia was the first of several women who performed these ritualistic predictions and prophesies, from the Oracle of Delphi. Visitors asked questions of the oracle, who considered Delphi as the center of the world. For more information see Jelle Zeilinga de Boer and John R. Hale. The Oracle of Delphi- Was She Really Stoned? *Biblical Archeology Society*, 17 July 2022. The Oracle of Delphi—Was She Really Stoned? - Biblical Archaeology Society

²²⁴ Ellen Duffer. As Artificial Intelligence Advances, What Are its Religious Implications? *Religion and Politics*. 29 August 2017. As Artificial Intelligence Advances, What Are its Religious Implications? | Religion & Politics (religionandpolitics.org)

Doomsday Predicted by AI

According to an apocalyptic prediction made by AI, the possibility of a nuclear war in the not-too-distant future is real. The prediction came with computer-generated pictures of desolate landscapes in the principal capitals around the world, including one of a mushroom cloud with the U.S. Capitol building and the Washington Monument in the background. The genesis of the speculation is directly tied to the demise of Vladimir Putin for starting the war against Ukraine, and the probability that he could press the nuclear button as his last act.[225] An article published three days later, on 2 January 2023, instead, explored Nostradamus prophecies for 2023. *Astrology vs Artificial Intelligence!* [226] The cryptic prophecies include a climate disaster with increased draught, great floods, social upheavals, revolution, riots, and a great war...

Michel de Nostredame
Nostradamus
1503-1566
Les Prophéties

Humans have a long history of worshipping the planets, the Sun, the Moon, animals, and other humans. Why not worship an AI-driven computer? What is the way of the future?[227] [228] As has been previously discussed in this book, AI results are not linked to ethics, morality, or religious convictions and practices. AI has no conscience. What is the *prediction* or the *prophecy* for a world in which technology becomes more and more ubiquitous with the passing of time? Are robots the next state or substitute for the priesthood? How will the different religious faiths react to AI, and how will they find a way to use it for their purposes? (This author is not willing to engage in competition with astrologers, forecasters, foretellers, prophets, seers, and soothsayers.)

---

[225] Henry Holloway. Mind of the Machine: Chilling AI predicts what nuclear war would look like with attacks on London, Moscow and Washington. *The Sun*. 31 December 2022. Chilling AI predicts what nuclear war would look like with attacks on London, Moscow and Washington | The US Sun (the-sun.com)

[226] Maariv Online. A great war, financial ruin and more: Nostradamus predictions for 2023. *The Jerusalem Post*. 2 January 2023. A great war, financial ruin and more: Nostradamus predictions for 2023 - The Jerusalem Post (jpost.com)

[227] Anjali UJ. Are artificial Intelligence and Religion Compatible? *Analytics Insight*. 28 May 2018. Are Artificial Intelligence and Religion Compatible? | Analytics Insight

[228] Shafi Musaddique. How artificial intelligence is shaping religion in the 21st century. CNBC. 11 May 2018. How artificial intelligence is shaping religion in the 21st century (cnbc.com)

Doomsday Clock Pushed Closer to Midnight

The idea of creating the so-called '*Doomsday Clock*' goes back to 1947, and was generated by an article published in *The Bulletin of the Atomic Scientists*. Among the scientists that came up with the concept were Albert Einstein (1878-1955), J. Robert Oppenheimer (1904-1967), and Eugene Rabinowitch (1901-1973). All three had participated in the Manhattan Project and been involved in the development of the first atomic bomb during WWII. They seem to show some remorse about participating in the invention of a nuclear bomb. The '*Doomsday Clock*,' encompasses a visual representation of how close the world is to a nuclear holocaust or global catastrophe due to a nuclear war. The 'clock' was set initially at seven minutes to midnight. During the Cold War, the clock was moved back and forth closer to midnight based on multiple doomsday scenarios. On 24 January 2022, as a result of the Russian invasion of Ukraine and fears of a Chinese mainland attack on Taiwan, a team of scientists made another adjustment, moving the clock closer to 90 seconds to midnight. It had never been placed any closer to *Doomsday*. There is an actual *Doomsday Clock*, resident at the University of Chicago.[229][230][231]

Albert Einstein, J. Robert Oppenheimer, and Eugene Rabinowitz

The concept is related to all the predictions of the four allegorical figures known as the *Four Horsemen of the Apocalypse*, predicting conquest by a foreign adversary, death, famine, pestilence, and war, and the cataclysmic destruction of the earth mentioned in the biblical *Book of Revelation* and ending with the battle of *Armageddon*.

---

[229] Louise Lerner. The Doomsday Clock, explained. *UChicago News*. What is the Doomsday Clock? | University of Chicago News (uchicago.edu)

[230] Gael Fashingbauer Cooper. Doomsday Clock Explained: How Close Are We to Armageddon in 2023? *CNET*. 24 January 2023. Doomsday Clock Explained: How Close Are We to Armageddon in 2023? – CNET

[231] Li Cohen. Doomsday clock hits 90 seconds to midnight as world gets closer to than ever to 'global catastrophe." *CBS News*. 24 January 2023. Doomsday clock hits 90 seconds to midnight as world gets closer than ever to "global catastrophe" - CBS News

Four Horsemen of the Apocalypse (1511)
Library of Congress Collection

Once you've lived the inside-out world of espionage, you never shed it. It's a mentality, a double standard of existence.

John le Carre

The habits and language of clandestinity can intoxicate even its practitioners.

William Colby

Deception: a Classic Weapon of Intelligence

> ***Intelligence* analysis:** a special or specific form of analysis normally carried out in a secret domain using special methodology and techniques to transform raw data into descriptions, explanations, and conclusions after considering multiple variables, for intelligence consumers, who normally are policy and decision-makers in a nation/state.
>
> **Studies in Intelligence,**
> **Vol. 47, No. 3, 2003**

A deception is an act or statement designed to *'mislead or create and promote a falsehood.'* The *Merriam-Webster Dictionary* defines deception as "*the act of causing someone to accept as true or valid what is false or invalid.*" Synonyms include *fraud, trickery, double-dealing, and subterfuge*. It is a form of entrapment. The term comes from the Medieval Latin *deceptionem*, and more recently from the French term *déception* or *décevoir*. It is a way to camouflage reality. Legally, it is a statutory *offense* to obtain something by telling false information, an untruth, or making a misrepresentation to mislead.

Deception has been a favorite weapon of war for a very long time. An example is a story described in Homer's ancient Greek epic poem the *Iliad*, which was written in the mid-8th Century BCE, considered to be the earliest work in the Western literary tradition. The Greeks had been laying siege to the walled city of Troy unsuccessfully for about ten years around the 12th Century BCE. They decided to build a wooden horse as a subterfuge, which they left outside the city walls. The Trojans believed that it was a kind of peace offering, and dragged it inside their walled city. It was packed with Greek warriors, who crept out in the middle of the night, killed the guards, and threw open the doors of the wall, and their army rushed in and captured the city.

AI: a Perfect Tool for Deception

In the arsenal of intelligence and counterintelligence operations, the *'art of deception and counter deception'* are critical tools that have deep historical roots. However, pinning down a definition of deception is not easy, particularly with the advent of AI. Deception, or *causing an individual to accept as true or valid what is false or invalid*, is the art of the *double-cross*. Even animals are known to use *'mimicry'* to deceive their prey or for self-defense. AI is a perfect tool to manipulate the perceptions of a person through *'deepfakes'* in video, audio, and images. AI can be used offensively, or defensively to detect deception by reading the emotions behind human expressions.[232] According to Dr. Heather Roff, Associate Research Fellow at the Leverhulme Center for the Future of Intelligence at the University of Cambridge, we need to have a robust understanding of all the ways AI could deceive, and *"some conceptual framework of the kinds of deceptions and AI agent may learn on its own before we can start proposing technological defenses."* [233]

Russia, for example, operates a *'troll farm'* that uses *'deepfakes'* and weaponized AI on international social media outlets, such as Facebook and Twitter during the 2016 U.S. elections.[234] It is suspected of disseminating and manipulating disinformation using WikiLeaks.[235] It is linked to Russia's Internet Research Agency (IRA). [236] Using AI, this organization created fake individuals and fake pictures, to tinker with elections in the U.S. and the UK, to dissuade voters to support left-wing candidates. Using AI, nation-states and cybercriminals can create realistic forgeries to spread disinformation, and manipulate elections. AI is also being used for 'distributed denial of service (DDoS)' through hacking of websites to make them inoperable, steal data, and interfere with elections. [237] [238] [239]

> A *'troll farm'* or *'troll factory,'* is an organization employing experts who work together across a distributed network to generate online traffic aimed at affecting public opinion by the deliberate spread of misinformation and disinformation.

---

[232] Heather Roff. AI Deception: When your artificial intelligence learns to lie. *CNAS.* 24 February 2020. AI Deception: When Your Artificial Intelligence Learns to Lie | Center for a New American Security (en-US) (cnas.org)

[233] Dr. Roth has also been a Research Associate at the Eisenhower Center for Space and Defense Studies at the United States Air Force Academy.

[234] Mike Snider. Robert Mueller investigation: What is a Russian troll farm" *USA Today.* 16 February 2018. Robert Mueller investigation, Donald Trump: What is a Russian troll farm? (usatoday.com)

[235] GhanaFact. Facebook report details how a Russia-linked troll farm was set up in Ghana to influence the 2020 US elections. *GhanaFact.* 1 June 2921. Facebook report details how a Russia-linked troll farm was set up in Ghana to influence the 2020 US elections - Ghana Fact

[236] Russia's most notorious troll farm reportedly used deepfakes to push a fake news outlet on Facebook. *Free Cape Cod News.* 2 September 2020. Russia's most notorious troll farm reportedly used deepfakes to push a fake news outlet on Facebook - FREE Cape Cod News

[237] Katyanna Quach. Deepfakes, quantum computing cracking codes, ransomware… Find out what's really freaking out Uncle Sam. *The Register.* 23 October 2019. Deepfakes, quantum computing cracking codes, ransomware… Find out what's really freaking out Uncle Sam • The Register

[238] Hannah Smith and Katherine Mansted. Weaponized deep fakes. *ASPI.* Weaponized deep fakes | Australian Strategic Policy Institute | ASPI

[239] Davey Alba. How Russia's Troll Farm Is Changing Tactics Before the Fall Elections. *The New York Times.* 29 March 2020. How Russia's Troll Farm Is Changing Tactics Before the Fall Election - The New York Times (nytimes.com)

AI: Multi-Disciplinary Approach for Deception

Current AI is based on multiple methods and motives, and the interdisciplinary work of experts from numerous disciplines, including sociologists, psychologists, political scientists, lawyers, military tacticians, and ethicists. Developing a comprehensive framework for AI deception is a complicated subject. AI deception includes acts of commission, actively sending misinformation, and acts of omission, where an AI is passive but is withholding information. AI can be used for all kinds of behaviors based on objective conditions.

AI can also be used to detect deception, for example, using biometrics, including facial recognition technology. It may bring about the end to traditional lying... For example, biometric systems and related AI technologies deployed at airports around the world can discover deceptive behavior and people trying to pass using false identities at high speed, and with greater accuracy than humans. Dishonesty has become a thing of the past with multiple measures using AI, for example, muscle movements, eye movements, and nervousness, in addition to enhanced fingerprint records, and multiple measurements using facial recognition. Noninvasive psychological profiling systems are already a fact of life, not speculation. Although some people continue to question the validity of multiple types of AI-powered detection systems, the fact is that they are very reliable. And AI-systems are already being used beyond airports by insurance companies, banks, and other private institutions to detect fraud.[240] [241] However, the advent of AI detection systems brings about the opposite reaction, as fraudsters try to invent countermeasures to beat the system. Without a doubt, the leading intelligence organizations around the world are already actively trying to come up with ways to defeat AI-powered detection systems, using AI for nefarious purposes. Historically, when an invention comes about, it triggers a counterreaction to defeat it with another invention, and that has always been a historical dilemma as technology does not necessarily live up to its promises.

AI: Open-Source Intelligence Collection and Analysis

What is *'open-source intelligence' (OSINT)?* It is intelligence gathered from the international news media and all types of resources publicly available. OSINT provides important information about why things happen, taking into account cultural differences, insight, and reflections on how and why people around the world think. *'Atmospherics,' 'perceptions,'* and *'emotions,'* are not the same in

---

[240] Adam Tanner. How Companies Are Using Artificial Intelligence to Tell if You're Lying. *Consumer Reports.* 9 November 2021.

[241] Louise Marie Jupe and David Adam Keatley. Airport artificial intelligence can detect deception: or am I lying? *SpringerLink.* 24 September 2019.

different parts of the globe.²⁴² More importantly, OSINT places in context intelligence gathered through traditional intelligence collection methods. In the digital age and with advances in AI, it is possible to collect and analyze a huge amount of data, to understand an adversary's goals, capabilities, intentions, and possible course of action.²⁴³

It is increasingly evident that OSINT research and analysis can produce results as good or better than traditional espionage in all its forms, from human intelligence (HUMIT) to all kinds of technological tools to intercept communications through the tools of the National Security Agency (NSA) and collect information through spy satellites using the tools of the National Geospatial-Intelligence Agency. All the tools of intelligence, surveillance, and reconnaissance (ISR) *are increasingly dependent on AI.* OSINT assisted by AI enhances collections and analysis using traditional tools of the intelligence community.

More advanced notice and warnings about very significant events are being mined through OSINT than through traditional tools of espionage.²⁴⁴ As has been disclosed multiple times to the news media, the CIA operates an Open-Source Enterprise and has been doing so for many years to carry out research and analysis, which obviously can be enhanced by AI. Everyone else around the globe, including our top competitors and friendly allied nations have been using OSINT for a long time. It is all about *competitive intelligence!*

AI-enhanced OSINT should be a close priority to HUMINT. It should be given proper funding. Espionage (intelligence) has been critical to national defense, as far back as the writings of Homer, Thucydides, Sun Tzu, Machiavelli, Clausewitz, and other great thinkers on the subject.²⁴⁵ The trick has always been to find out about the enemies' intentions to gain the advantage.

---

[242] Loren Blinde. Why We Need Open-Source Intelligence. Intelligencecommunitynews.com 15 September 2020. Why We Need Open-Source Intelligence - Intelligence Community News

[243] Bon Ashley and Neil Wiley. How the Intelligence Community Can Get Better at Open-Source Intel. *Defense One.* 16 July 2021. How the Intelligence Community Can Get Better at Open-Source Intel - Defense One

[244] Nomaan Merchant. US spies lag rivals in seizing on data hiding in plain sight. *Associated Press News.* 12 January 2023. US spies lag rivals in seizing on data hiding in plain sight | AP News

[245] Crispin Burke. Sun-Tzu, Clausewitz, and Thucydides: It's Only a Lot of Reading If You Do It. Thestrategicbridge.org. 13 February 2014. Sun-Tzu, Clausewitz, and Thucydides: It's Only a Lot of Reading If You Do It (thestrategybridge.org)

DECEPTION HAS BEEN AROUND FOR A VERY LONG TIME

Guido de Columna. *Historia Destructionis Troiae*. Augsburg. 1488.
Library of Congress Collection

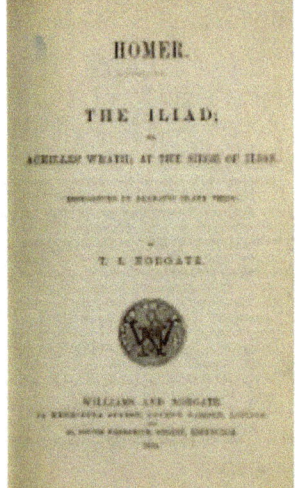 

Even a fool may be wise after the event.

Homer, *The Iliad*

We must set aside old notions and embrace fresh ones; and, as we learn, we must be daily unlearning something that has cost us no small labor and anxiety to acquire.

Homer, *The Iliad*

Trojans and Achaeans, who like wolves sprang upon one another, with man against man in the onfall.

Homer, *The Iliad*

The War-God has no favorites: he has been known to kill the man who thought he was going to do the killing...

Homer, *The Iliad*

Weaponizing Artificial Intelligence (AI)

AI resembles a 3-dimensional chess game with the arrival of innovative algorithms which allow pieces to move between multiple game boards. The new rules of warfare cannot cover all the possible situations that can arise, resulting in a game that is so complex, that it is not recognizable by a human. The new reality is tough and deceptive, and there are no enforceable rules. Players have to think thousands of moves ahead, and nobody knows what the endgame looks like, or if it is possible for a player to win in this game.

A *'weapon'* is an instrument, or any type of physical device, used in combat, or a psychological instrument of attack or defense. Weapons have been used since the Stone Age by early humans for various purposes, but mainly to cause injury, or defeat an enemy. In a broader sense, a weapon is *'anything that can be used to gain material, mental, strategic or tactical advantage over an adversary, including AI, that can be used to target human and non-human adversaries.'* There are many types of weapons designed to inflict bodily damage on an adversary. Among the types of weapons are toxic and biological substances, including artificially manufactured toxic substances, and they can all be enhanced by AI.

All weapons are generally regulated by national or federal law, as well as local, municipal, provincial, or state laws. There are also international conventions on acceptable rules of warfare, and *'acceptable'* weapons systems. Anti-personnel mines, booby traps, incendiary weapons that target civilians, laser weapons that can permanently blind, chemical weapons, and cluster bombs, are banned, but so far, there are no bans on weaponized AI systems. More than 30 countries have called for a ban on fully autonomous weapons systems, but there are no current controls on their use.

Weapons may be classified as *offensive* or *defensive. Among the many types of weapons are clubs, blades, blackjacks,* daggers, knives, brass knuckles, metal pipes, pistols, razors, and revolvers. Carrying concealed weapons is illegal in most jurisdictions worldwide. Since antiquity, there have been regulations to regulate the possession and use of weapons. There is no practical way to regulate or control AI. There are already multiple types of weapons powered by AI that are capable of 'thinking' and acting on their own and hitting their selected targets without human interaction.[246] [247]

---

[246] Gerrit De Vynck. The U.S. says humans will always be in control of AI weapons. But the age of autonomous war is already here. *The Washington Post.* 7 July 2021. Autonomous weapons already exist and are playing a role on battlefields like Libya and Armenia - The Washington Post

[247] Frank Pasquale. 'Machines set loose to slaughter ': the dangerous rise of military AI. *The Guardian.* 15 October 2020. 'Machines set loose to slaughter': the dangerous rise of military AI | Artificial intelligence (AI) | The Guardian

Like any other array of technologies and disciplines in information technology (IT), AI *'weapons'* are not immune to manipulation by malware, bugs, and hacking. AI weapons are subsets of IT. AI weapons systems are purpose-built machines or software designed to perform as weapons that can be programmed for specific tasks. They represent the application of AI to create autonomous machines (*robots)* that are capable of carrying out a complex series of actions automatically and can learn and apply knowledge in a similar way that humans and animals think, learn, make decisions, and act.

AI is currently being used for multiple scientific research tasks, including studies of human genes, with the potential to create "superior" genetically designed soldiers. Ethical concerns do not seem to be given a prominent consideration as AI gets weaponized.[248] Machines do not have morals or values, and their decision-making process does not include deciding right and wrong based on any ethical considerations. The key players in AI are the U.S., China, Russia, the UK, France, Israel, and South Korea.[249] People in these countries have their views on ethics, which they redefined to handle any situation.[250]

Before the Russian invasion of Ukraine on 24 February 2022, the advent of weaponized artificial intelligence was in the realm of speculation. There were reports here and there about how several countries were updating their weapons systems by enhancing them with AI. After the start of the conflict, the creative ability of Ukrainian *Freedom Fighters,* moved AI into a new era of enhanced weapons systems, from the fairly simple to a new frontier in warfare. The Russian military leadership had a clash with reality. Weaponized AI does not work always as intended, and it is no substitute for common sense.

---

[248] Jayshree Pandya. *Forbes* 14 January 2019. The Weaponization of Artificial Intelligence (forbes.com)

[249] Kirsten Gronlund. State of AI: Artificial Intelligence, the Military and Increasingly Autonomous Weapons. *Future of Life.* 9 May 2019. State of AI: Artificial Intelligence, the Military and Increasingly Autonomous Weapons - Future of Life Institute

[250] Japanese leaders decided to attack the American naval base at Pearl Harbor on 7 December 1941, with their own ethical justification, without first declaring war, and American leadership used their own set of ethical standards to drop two atomic bombs and kill thousands of non-combatant civilians in Japanese cities in 1945 to end WWII.

Braggadocio Before the Russian-Ukraine War in 2022

Weaponized AI Without Arrogance: Israeli Style

In May 2021, Israeli Defense Forces (IDF) used the first ever "*drone swarm*" in a battle to hunt down Hamas terrorists in the Gaza Strip. The drones do not have human input, but instead '*link together using AI to seek out targets that have been programmed.*' Israel did not use ground forces, and instead used swarms of drones, demonstrating the growth of autonomy and machine-to-machine collaboration in warfare without the need for an operator. The drones were fed data from satellites, other reconnaissance drones, other aerial vehicles, and ground-collected intelligence. Israel has not confirmed the particulars of how these operations were carried out.[251] Without a doubt, the IDF has made significant progress in the weaponization of AI, but they do not engage in braggadocio.

Weaponized AI With Arrogance and Cockiness: Chinese Style

According to the official Chinese military newspaper _PLA Daily_ published in June 2021, China's AI fighter jet pilots are now '*better than humans.*' Chinese fighter pilots have been going up against aircraft piloted by artificial intelligence and can shoot them down in simulated dogfights. According to the article, a People's Liberation Army Air Force brigade flight team leader and recognized fighter ace, Fang Guoyu, was recently "shot down" by a robotic AI fighter jet pilot on simulated air-to-air combat. The AI pilot learned from its human opponent with each simulated battle, and using the same technique Fan Guoyu had used defeated him.[252] In another article in the _South China Morning Post_, the Chinese military has another 'top secret' AI-based weapon system that can track and blast enemy submarines with no human input. The Chinese military 'revealed' that it has been working on this technology since the 1990s, and has been testing since 2010 an underwater drone (or underwater attack robot torpedo), designed to track and destroy enemy submarines without the need for human input.[253]

---

[251] Tariq Tahir. SEEK AND DESTROY - Israel uses first-ever AI drone swarm in battle to hunt down and blitz Hamas terrorists with NO human input. The U.S. Sun. 5 July 2021. Israel uses first-ever AI drone swarm in battle to hunt down and blitz Hamas terrorists with NO human input (the-sun.com)

[252] Olivia Burke. Terminated China's AI fighter jet pilots are now 'better than humans' and can shoot them down in dogfights. The Sun. 16 June 2021. https://www.the-sun.com/news/us-news/3094519/chinas-ai-fighter-jet-pilots-better-humans-dogfights/

[253] Felix Allen. DRONE WARS- China reveals top secret AI drone that can track & blast enemy submarines with NO human input. The US Sun. 8 July 2021. https://www.the-sun.com/news/3244994/china-top-secret-underwater-drone/

China is the top economic and military competitor for the U.S., and a real threat to American military technology, particularly in the weaponization of AI.[254] In July 2017, the Chinese State Council issued its AI development plan: *New Generation Artificial Intelligence Development Plan* (AIDP). This plan outlines the Chinese goals:

> *AI has become a new focus of international competition. AI is a strategic technology that will lead in the future; the world's major developed countries are taking the development of AI as a major strategy to enhance national competitiveness and protect national security.*[255]

In October 2018, Major General Ding Xiangrong, Deputy Director of the General Office of China's Central Military Commission further defined China's goals in AI: *"narrow the gap between the Chinese military and global advanced powers" by taking advantage of the "ongoing military revolution . . . centered on information technology and intelligent technology."*[256] Chinese leaders have taken steps to eliminate competition in AI, by keeping foreign companies out of their domestic market, including the leading American companies in the field. China is restricting exports of innovative AI technology, even though several Chinese companies are world leaders, including Alibaba, Baidu, ByteDance, Douyin, Tencent, and TikTok. Technology linked to the weaponization of AI is fiercely protected.[257] According to a published DOD analysis, China has moved to *'intelligentize'* warfare.[258] [259]

The PRC wants to project power globally and to achieve that goal, they are enhancing military information systems across the board. Among the key PRC efforts to weaponize AI are such things as unmanned aerial vehicles (UAVs), ocean surface(USVs), and underwater vehicles (UUVs) They are also working on the development of hypersonic missiles and hypervelocity weapons systems, as well as weapons that allow long-distance striking of targets. They are engaged in refining and expanding their space-based capabilities, and modernizing their air

---

[254] Rise of Chinese artificial intelligence (AI) and quantum computing a threat to U.S. military technology. *Military & Aerospace Electronics*. 9 September 2020. Rise of Chinese artificial intelligence (AI) and quantum computing a threat to U.S. military technology | Military Aerospace

[255] Gregory C. Allen. Understanding China's AI Strategy. CNAS. 6 February 2019. Understanding China's AI Strategy | Center for a New American Security (en-US) (cnas.org)

[256] Ibid.

[257] Bernard Marr. China Poised to Dominate the Artificial Intelligence (AI) Market. *Forbes*. 15 March 2021. China Poised to Dominate the Artificial Intelligence (AI) Market (forbes.com)

[258] Mark Pomerleau. China moves toward new 'intelligentized' approach to warfare, says Pentagon. C4isrnet.com. 1 September 2020. China moves toward new 'intelligentized' approach to warfare, says Pentagon (c4isrnet.com)

[259] DOD. Military and Security Developments Involving the People's Republic of China 2020: Annual Report to Congress. *U.S. Department of Defense*. 2020 China Military Power Report (defense.gov)

force with next-generation planes. For example, they are working on a stealth nuclear-capable bomber, the H-20, as well as advanced fighter planes (J-20 Chengdu). According to published reports, the H-20 looks like the U.S. B-2 Spirit bomber and reportedly will have a long reach.[260] All of these efforts are supported by extensive espionage in all its forms. Chinese intercontinental ballistic missiles (ICBMs) with multiple nuclear warheads are already a reality.[261]

The U.S. F-22 Raptor, manufactured by Lockheed Martin, is regarded as the best fighter in the world as of February 2023, there are problems ahead. The Chinese are rapidly increasing the size of their fleet of Chengdu J-20 *Mighty Dragon* Stealth Fighter, and are expected to overtake the U.S. in the number of available fighters. The F-22 is a very expensive aircraft, which has limited its production. Based on open-source reporting, the U.S. only has about 187 operational F-22 fighters. The U.S. is increasing the number of F-35s, but not at the speed that the Chinese Air Force is expanding its fleet.[262] The estimated size of the *People's Liberation Army Air Force* as of February 2023, is estimated at 3,284, compared to about 13,300 aircraft in the U.S. arsenal and about 4,182 in Russia's arsenal (except they are losing assets every day in their war against Ukraine.)[263] The issue is not numbers but the quality of the technology and operational capabilities. AI plays a key role in air power. It is estimated that about 1700 military airplanes are operational.

China acquired nuclear weapons in 1964. Since then, Key Chinese military equipment, including nuclear weapons and delivery systems were enhanced by American secrets stolen through traditional espionage assisted by advanced IT, and AI. Some of the Chinese advances in military technology are without a doubt a result of American-Chinese cooperation in the 1990s.[264] According to Admiral Charles Richard, who commanded U.S. nuclear forces until 9 December 2022, Chinese nuclear forces exceeded those of the U.S. for the first time in one of three areas: warheads, long-range missiles, and launchers. He repeated this assessment for over a year before his tenure in that important position. For

---

[260] Kris Osborn. China's New H-20 Stealth Bomber: Just a Copycat of the B-2 Spirit? *MSN*. 16 March 2023. China's New H-20 Stealth Bomber: Just a Copycat of the B-2 Spirit? (msn.com)

[261] Maya Carlin. H-20 Stealth Bomber: A Threat to the U.S. Military or Flying Paper Tiger? *MSN*. 23 February 2023. China's H-20 Stealth Bomber: A Threat to the U.S. Military or Flying Paper Tiger? (msn.com)

[262] Peter Suciu. China's J-20 Stealth Fighter Has One Big Advantage Over America. *MSN.Com*. 16 February 2023. China's J-20 Stealth Fighter Has One Big Advantage over America (msn.com) 15 May 2020.

[263] 2023 China Military Strength. 2023 China Military Strength (globalfirepower.com)

[264] Bill Gertz. Beijing spies stole bomb secrets on every U.S. warhead to build nuclear forces. *The Washington Times*.3 January 2023. China's nuclear forces built in part with U.S. technology - Washington Times

example, he pointed out that Chinese intercontinental ballistic missiles (ICBMs) were capable of carrying multiple nuclear warheads to their targets.[265] A similar warning had been made by Defense Intelligence Agency (DIA) Lt. Gen. Robert P. Ashley in 2019.[266] *But how did the PRC diversify and expand its nuclear arsenal using advanced technology? How come it took so long for the U.S. to understand that Chinese policy was shifting to one of preparing for coercive international politics by the threat of nuclear war?*

As of the school year 2010-2011, there were an estimated 157,558 Chinese college and university students going to school in the U.S. By the school year 2019-2020, the number had increased to at least 372,532 students. With the start of the COVID pandemic, the numbers dropped in the school year 2020-2021 to about 317,299.[267] As of the latest statistics during the school year 2021-2022, about 22.2% were studying mathematics and computer sciences, followed by about 17.5% studying engineering.[268] There is considerable evidence that an undetermined number of these students have been involved in espionage to steal American technology.[269] An undetermined number of these students opted to remain in the U.S. and obtain American citizenship and volunteered to enter the U.S. Armed Forces. A considerable number of these "students" eventually became employed as U.S. Defense contractors. *What percentage of these "students" were recruited into Chinese intelligence before they even applied to go to school in the U.S.?* There is considerable evidence in open source about how the Chinese Government has also harassed Chinese living in the U.S. to enlist them in espionage.[270]

Over time, the sophistication of Chinese espionage operations have increased substantially, adding AI to traditional espionage tools. They continuously engage in the theft of American intellectual property, targeting

---

[265] Patty-Jane Geller. China's Nuclear Expansion and its Implications for U.S. Strategy and Security. *The Heritage Foundation.* 14 September 2022. China's Nuclear Expansion and its Implications for U.S. Strategy and Security | The Heritage Foundation

[266] Rebeccah L. Heinrichs. China's Destabilizing nuclear weapons 'Strategic Breakout.' *Hudson Institute.* 8 September 2021. China's Destabilizing nuclear weapons 'Strategic Breakout' | Hudson

[267] C. Textor. Number of college and university students from China in the United States from academic year 2020/11 to 2020/21. *Statista.* 27 July 2022. Number of Chinese students in the U.S. 2021 | Statista

[268] C. Textor. Study field distribution of Chinese students in the United States in academic year 2020/21. *Statista.* 26 November 2021. Chinese students in the U.S. by subject 2021 | Statista

[269] Zachary Cohen and Alex Marquardt. US intelligence warns China is using student spies to steal secrets. *CNN.* 1 February 2019. US intelligence warns China using student spies to steal secrets | CNN Politics

[270] Kai Suherwan. The Dragon's Reach: Chinese Espionage Operations in the United States. *The Sycamore Institute.* 2 July 2022. The Dragon's Reach: Chinese Espionage Operations in the United States (sycamoreinstitute.org)

high-tech areas, particularly IT. Cyber espionage enhanced with AI is without a doubt a primary means to collect secrets. Although it is practically impossible to put a price tag on Chinese economic espionage, it has been estimated to top $320 billion by 2018. The cumulative impact of economic espionage has been estimated to amount to trillions of dollars. Among the areas targeted by China are robotics, avionics, '*hypersonics*,' and AI.[271]

One critical example of how dysfunctional American and ally export controls are, was the continued use by Chinese military labs, including nuclear weapons researchers, of imported semiconductors from Intel and Nvidia, despite export bans in existence since at least 1997. In 2022, the U.S. Government took steps to tighten up the regulations and export controls, but it may have been too little too late.[272] Back in the 1930's Japan was able to purchase scrap steel and other strategic materials from the U.S. despite everyone knowing full well that they were building their military and getting ready to go to war. All the scrap iron and steel were returned to the U.S. in the form of bullets during WWII. Some people find it very difficult to learn lessons from history, including American political leaders. The average American teenager upon graduating from High School has a very shallow knowledge of world history, as compared to secondary school students in other countries.[273]

---

[271] Nicholas Eftimiades. The Impact of Chinese Espionage on the United States. *The Diplomat.* 4 December 2018. The Impact of Chinese Espionage on the United States – The Diplomat

[272] Liza Lin and Dan Strumpf. China's Top Nuclear-Weapons Lab Used American Computer Chips Decades After Ban. *Wall Street Journal.* 29 January 2023. China's Top Nuclear-Weapons Lab Used American Computer Chips Decades After Ban – WSJ

[273] Drew Desilver. U.S. Students' academic achievement still lags that of their peers in many other countries. *Pew Research Center.* 15 February 2017. U.S. academic achievement lags that of many other countries | Pew Research Center

> All warfare is based on deception. Hence, when we are able to attack, we must seem unable; when using our forces, we must appear inactive; when we are near, we must make the enemy believe we are far away; when far away, we must make him believe we are near.

**THE ART OF WAR
SUN TZU
(770-476 BC)
Chinese Strategic Culture on the use of Deception, Espionage, Intelligence, Psychological Warfare**

Chinese weaponizing of Artificial Intelligence (AI) in all its forms – from biometrics to weapons systems - presents an unprecedented danger to the world

People's Republic of China – Air Force Aircraft as of 2023 (Estimate)

Airplane	Type		Compare with U.S. Air Power
Chengdu J-10A	4th Generation Multi-role Fighter (2004)	About 240 of the different variants of the J-10 are estimated to be flying as of 2023	F-16 Fighting Falcon (Multiple variants available)
Chengdu J-10B	Multi-role Fighter (2014)	Updated avionics, Active Electronically Scanned Array radar	
Chengdu J-10C	Multi-role Fighter (2021)	Incorporated a domestically produced engine-	
Chengdu Black Eagle J-20	5th generation – stealth multirole fighter (2017)	China may have about 150 operational fighters of this type	F-35 5th generation fighter
Shenyang J-11	Used by the Chinese Air Force and Navy	Airframe derived from Russian Sukhoi Su-27 – About 255 of these aircraft have been produced	
Shenyang J-15	5th generation fighter – has landed successfully on the aircraft carrier Liaoning (2013?)	These fighters are operational on the aircraft carriers Liaoning and Shandong.	
Shenyang J-16	(2015) 4th generation multirole strike fighter	Derived from Russia's Sukhoi Su-27	
Shenyang FC-31	5th generation fighter – reportedly uses American technology linked to the F-35, obtained through espionage -	These fighters may replace the Shenyang J-15 for use in the two Chinese aircraft carriers.	F-35 5th generation fighter
Gongji-11 GJ-11	Unmanned stealth combat aerial vehicle (UCAV) (2019)	Technology from Northrop Grumman's X, (47B) may have been stolen and incorporated into this UCAV Source: https://tvd.im/aviation/896-gongji-11-gj-11.html	
H-20	Stealth strategic bomber (Operational in 2025?)	Intercontinental power-projection capability with range, speed, stealth, and capability of carrying 45 tons of bombs for over 7,000 miles	Timeline for production similar to the American B-21

Multiple sources used - [274] [275] [276]

---

[274] Active Chinese Air Force Aircraft (2023). Militaryfactory.com. Active Chinese Air Force Aircraft (2023) (militaryfactory.com)

[275] The 11 Best Chinese Fighter Jets of the PLA Air Force. Aerocorner. The 11 Best Chinese Fighter Jets of the PLA Air Force - Aero Corner

[276] H-20 Stealth Bomber: Is China's latest firepower overhyped? *Asianet*. 28 February 2023. H-20 Stealth Bomber: Is China's latest firepower overhyped? (msn.com)

Weaponized AI With Bombast: Russian Style

Russia was building an Army of AI weapons to meet various combat needs and was rapidly "advancing" to meet this goal.[277] [278] [279] For example, they were working on an unmanned version of the Armata T-14 Main Battle Tank, which was expected to make use of AI, as part of the effort to carry out remote-control operations in combat. According to Russian state media, the Armata T-14 will be the first tank in the world to incorporate 'network-centric warfare.'[280] It was expected to enter service in 2022. With AI technology, these tanks may be able to make their own decisions to fire on a target. Russia was also working on other autonomous weapons, including a remote-controlled Su-57 5th generation multi-role fighter jet.[281] The Russians were suggesting that a 6th-generation fighter jet could be developed shortly, and they were systematically copying American AI robotics. They were also developing unmanned underwater/surface vehicles for the Russian Navy (UUV/USV).[282] [283] And then, the bombastic braggadocio had a clash with reality.

The T-14 Armata clashed with reality as Russia invaded Ukraine in 2022. It simply flopped. It turns out that it is expensive to manufacture, with an estimated cost of between $4 and $6 million, and there are no spare parts. And according to published reports, maintenance crews not only lack spare parts but are not trained to return them to combat. In addition, it is too heavy and hard to transport, and unable to function properly in mud. In addition, it uses a significant amount of imported technology. Despite all the propaganda about producing 2,300 units by 2025, only about 100 were available when the war

---

[277] Tom O'Connor. Russia is building an Army of robot weapons, and China's AI tech is helping. *Newsweek*. 24 May 2021. Russia Is Building an Army of Robot Weapons, and China's AI Tech Is Helping (newsweek.com)

[278] Samuel Bendett. The Rise of Russia's Hi-Tech Military. *American Foreign Policy Council*. 26 June 2019. Articles | American Foreign Policy Council (afpc.org)

[279] Andrew Eversden. AZ warning to DoD: Russia advances quicker than expected on AI, battlefield tech. C4SRnet. 24 May 2021. A warning to DoD: Russia advances quicker than expected on AI, battlefield tech (c4isrnet.com)

[280] Christina Kitova. Russia Developing AI Tech in Tanks. *Communal News*. 26 February 2021. Russia Developing AI Tech in Tanks - Communal News: Online Business, Wholesale & B2B Marketplace News

[281] Peter Suciu. Is Russia Developing an Unmanned Armata T-14 Tank? *National Interest*. 24 August 2020. Is Russia Developing an Unmanned Armata T-14 Tank? | The National Interest

[282] Peter Suciu. Russia's Sixth-Generation Stealth Fighter Could Use Artificial Intelligence Weapons. National Interest. 3 October 2020. Russia's Sixth-Generation Stealth Fighter Could Use Artificial Intelligence Weapons | The National Interest

[283] George Gilder. Russia is systematically copying U.S. military AI Robotics. *Mind Matters*. 15 October 2021. Russia Is Systematically Copying U.S. Military AI Robotics | Mind Matters

started in February 2022.²⁸⁴ They were not sent into combat for multiple reasons. Russians are great at producing *deception, information warfare,* and *psychological warfare...* their problem is that they seem to *deceive themselves* by believing their propaganda. (In the vernacular, one would say that it is stupid to believe your own *heifer dust-* - a polite way of saying bulls---.)

Russia's AI strategy was outlined by the President of the Russian Federation Vladimir Putin in a decree issued on 27 February 2019.²⁸⁵ He ordered state-owned companies to take the lead in a high-priority effort to develop AI and make Russia the international leader. In October 2019, Russia made public its national AI strategy, in which they outline its plans to step up scientific R&D in AI, but without setting specific deadlines or metrics to assess their progress.²⁸⁶ ²⁸⁷ ²⁸⁸ ²⁸⁹

The nation that leads in AI
"Will become the ruler of the world"
September 2017

Russia had been developing autonomous weapons platforms using AI, trying to catch up with the U.S. to achieve information dominance, and mimicking Chinese efforts in AI. They may be cooperating with China in weaponizing AI, but they share a long border, and there are limits to their cooperation, considering the long history of border conflicts between the two countries.²⁹⁰ The last Sino-Soviet border conflict took place in 1969 when PLA troops attacked Soviet border guards on Zhenbao Island. The incident caused at least 58 Soviet casualties and at least 29 Chinese casualties. However actual losses on both sides may have been considerably higher.

Putin placed state-owned bank Sberbank in charge of funding AI research. Russia, like other countries, is investing in unmanned and robotic platforms that are based on AI, as well as in developing countermeasures for these types of

---

[284] Brent M. Eastwood. Russia's T-14 Armata: The 'Super' Tank That Flopped in Ukraine? *MSN.com.* 5 January 2023. Russia's T-14 Armata: The 'Super' Tank That Flopped in Ukraine? (msn.com)

[285] Ryan Daws. Putin outlines Russia's national AI strategy priorities. *AI News.* 31 May 2019.

[286] Andrew S. Bowen. Russian Armed Forces: Military Doctrine and Strategy. *Congressional Research Service.* 20 August 2020. Russian Armed Forces: Military Doctrine and Strategy (congress.gov)

[287] Margarita Konaev. Thoughts on Russia's AI Strategy. *CSET* (Georgetown University). 30 October 2019. Thoughts on Russia's AI Strategy - Center for Security and Emerging Technology (georgetown.edu)

[288] Samuel Bendett. Russia's AI Quest is State-Driven – Even More than China's. Can It Work? *Defense One.* 25 November 2019. Russia's AI Quest is State-Driven — Even More than China's. Can It Work? - Defense One

[289] Samuel Bendett. Russia's National AI Center Is Taking Shape. Op. Cit.

[290] Tom O'Connor. Russia Is Building an Army of Robot Weapons, and China's AI Tech is Helping. *Newsweek.* 24 May 2021. Russia Is Building an Army of Robot Weapons, and China's AI Tech Is Helping (newsweek.com)

weapons systems. An important component in these efforts is the perceived future role of human control vs. independent systems that can think and act on their own using AI. Intelligence, Surveillance, and Reconnaissance (ISR) provide the foundation for all military operations, and they are increasingly dependent on AI.[291] [292] On 10 October 2019, Russia made public its 10-year national plan with the vision to become the world leader in AI. Although the plan did not focus directly on the military use of AI, it included the priority goal of taking the lead in command and control, communications, intelligence, surveillance, and reconnaissance capabilities.[293] [294]

Russia's AI research and development (R&D) seems to be centered at the Moscow Institute of Physics and Technologies (MIPT), which is hosting several known projects related to speech recognition and machine learning technologies.[295] Russia operates another campus on the Black Sea Coast, where civilian and military experts work on AI-supported projects.[296] Russia's Chief of the General Staff, Valery Gerasimov, has repeatedly described a new concept of the '*nature of war in modern times*,' and in line with President Putin's view that whoever becomes dominant in AI, will control the world.

Russian semi-autonomous robot tanks using AI were utterly useless in Syria, and their experience in Ukraine is not much better.

---

[291] Raytheon. How artificial intelligence and machine learning will make ISR faster. *Raytheon Intelligence & Space*. 3 September 2020. How artificial intelligence and machine learning will make ISR faster - Smart software can exponentially accelerate threat response | Raytheon Intelligence & Space (raytheonintelligenceandspace.com)

[292] Jon Harper. Artificial Intelligence to Sort Through ISR Data Glut. *National Defense*. 16 January 2028. Artificial Intelligence to Sort Through ISR Data Glut (nationaldefensemagazine.org)

[293] Margarita Konaev. Thoughts on Russia's AI Strategy. *CSET*. 30 October 2019. Thoughts on Russia's AI Strategy - Center for Security and Emerging Technology (georgetown.edu)

[294] Stephanie Petrella, Chris Miller, Benjamin Cooper. Russia's Artificial Intelligence Strategy: The Role of State-Owned Firms. *Science Direct*. Vol. 65. 24 December 2020.
[295] Samuel Bendett. Russia's National AI Center Is Taking Shape. Defense One. 27 September 2019. Russia's National AI Center Is Taking Shape - Defense One

[296] George Gilder. Russia is Systematically Copying U.S. Military AI Robotics. Mindmatters. 15 October 2020. Russia Is Systematically Copying U.S. Military AI Robotics | Mind Matters

Weaponized AI With Caveats: American Style

The U.S. was and continues to be the leading country in AI in general, and in the weaponization of AI in particular, before Russia invaded Ukraine.[297] The PRC is making inroads, but it is far from catching up to the U.S. EU-member states lag. American IT experts, R&D, and hardware put the U.S. in the first place, particularly in weaponized AI. The U.S. enjoys the best climate for private sector entrepreneurs to be creative and start companies that introduce new ideas, including new AI-based products. Not only does the U.S. has the best talent, but it also functions like a magnet that attracts talent from all over the world. In the past few years, some people have questioned the U.S.'s ability to maintain the lead in AI, but despite some gloom and doom on the subject, American technology continues to lead the way.[298] [299] The top AI companies continue to be American.

The U.S. National Security Commission on Artificial Intelligence (NSCAI) released its Final Report to Congress and the President on 1 March 2021. The NSCAI recommended the responsible development and use of AI technologies to protect national security. It suggested that the Intelligence Community and the Department of Defense actively participate in the global technology competition to defend the interests of the country. It suggested that the talent pool be expanded by educating more young people in IT. It suggested that additional investments be made in R&D, and that Congress in 2022 enacted legislation to that effect.[300] Billions of dollars will be invested to expand chip manufacturing in the U.S., in part through the Infrastructure Investment and Jobs Act, which will provide $289 billion in the CHIPS and Science Act. The NSCAI report also suggested reinvigorating alliances to expand the interoperability of defense capabilities, including AI-enabled and emerging technologies. (Plenty of gobbledygook and gibberish in government reports that are representative of the political culture.)

---

[297] Sintia Radu. Despite Chinese Efforts, the U.S. Still Leaders in AI. *U.S. News*. 19 August 2019. The U.S. Is Still the Global Leader in Artificial Intelligence (usnews.com)

[298] Will Knight. The U.S. Leads in Artificial Intelligence, but for How Long. *MIT Technology Review* 6 December 2017. The U.S. Leads in Artificial Intelligence, but for How Long? | MIT Technology Review

[299] Liam Tung. Who leads the world on AI? A decade from now, it might not be the US. *ZDNet.com*. 2 March 2021. Who leads the world on AI? A decade from now, it might not be the US | ZDNET

[300] David Rotman. 2022's seismic shift in US tech policy will change how we innovate. *MIT Technology Review*. 9 January 2023. 2022's seismic shift in US tech policy will change how we innovate | MIT Technology Review

Russian-Ukraine War

> Relatively small countries can make up for their deficiencies with superior intelligence and ingenuity.
> **Allen Dulles**
> **(1893-1969)**[301]

One of the most significant aspects of the Russia-Ukraine War is the miscalculations about the expected outcome made by both sides and outside observers. They left out *"inconvenient"* truths about objective conditions related to Ukrainian nationalism, leadership, and technological know-how. The invasion should not have been a surprise to anyone, considering that Russia invaded Georgia in 2008, Vladimir Putin annexed Crimea in 2014 and fomented rebellion in Eastern Ukraine, namely in Donbas, Donetsk, and Luhansk.[302]

International observers miscalculated the potential outcome of the Russian invasion of Ukraine on February 24, 2022, particularly doubting the Ukrainian ability to fight for their country against all odds, including some of the most savage and barbarous weapons ever devised. Putin in particular made a disastrous miscalculation when he crossed the border into Ukraine, thinking it was going to be a simple operation to defeat the Ukrainians and start rebuilding the old Soviet Union.[303] Too many people, not just Vladimir Putin, made the wrong assumptions, particularly, that Volodymyr Zelenskyy was not up to the task. Instead, the Russian military bleed in Ukraine, suffering very heavy casualties, and President Putin became a global pariah.

These are some important facts about Ukraine. The country has a population of about 41.5 million, which makes it the eighth-most populous country in Europe. It is the second-largest country in Europe after Russia, with an area of 233,062 square miles. It had the third-largest armed forces in Europe after Russia and France. Ukraine ranked before the war as one of the world's top 12 weapons exporters.[304] Despite being divided multiple times in the past 800 years among its neighbors and regional empires, including Austria-Hungary, the Ottoman Empire, Russia, and the Soviet Union, Ukrainian nationalism is a fact of life. Since gaining independence in 1991, after the breakup of the Soviet

---

[301] Director, Central Intelligence (1953-1961).

[302] Russia also intervened in the Syrian Civil War in 2015 and continues to provide military support for the Syrian dictator.

[303] Roman Goncharenko. Russia's Ukraine war based on 'a disastrous miscalculation.' *Deutsche Well*. Russia's Ukraine war based on 'a disastrous miscalculation' (msn.com)

[304] Vitaliy Goncharuk. Ukraine's roadmap to an artificial intelligence future. *Atlantic Council*. 19 January 2021. Ukraine's roadmap to an artificial intelligence future - Atlantic Council

Union, Ukrainian nationalism continued to grow, despite multiple challenges, including a high poverty rate and considerable corruption.[305]

The Russia-Ukraine war became a test site for AI technology created in multiple countries.[306] The war has been described primarily as a *"battle of drones."* For example, advanced drones manufactured in Turkey have been used to drop laser-guided ammunition on Russian military targets. Iranian-manufactured drones have been used by Russia as *'kamikaze drones'* against Ukrainian targets.[307] The use of *"killer robot"* technology has been used by both sides. Both, autonomous and uncrewed military weapons, such as those that use AI have been frequently used by Russia and Ukraine, contributing to the proliferation of the technology worldwide. Every day that passes, both sides come up with new ways of weaponizing AI. One of the most interesting developments is that both sides are placing bounties on captured AI weapons systems. For example, the Russians placed a one-million-ruble bounty on any German-built THeMIS units captured from the Ukrainians.[308] Despite the use of weaponized AI, conventional weapons played a key role in the outcome.

Conventional Weapons

The losses suffered by Russia in conventional military equipment are staggering. According to general wisdom before the war, Russia had the second most powerful military in the world. Russian leaders had a nasty awakening when their image of a superpower clashed with reality after they invaded Ukraine on 24 February 2022. There are self-evident facts about the serious design flaws of Russian military equipment, particularly in tank design. They lost a huge number of tanks in the first ten months of the war. For example, ammunition storage in Russian tanks was put in the wrong place, and not properly protected.[309] The most advanced tank – the T-90M - did not do well in combat, despite advanced armor protection and other features. The Russian military quickly used a large

Largest Donors of Military Equipment to Ukraine
The U.S.
Germany
UK
Poland
Canada
Netherlands
Italy
Latvia
Turkey
Estonia
France
Australia
Norway

---

[305] Artificial Intelligence in Ukraine. *Rebellionresearch.com*. 17 March 2021. Artificial Intelligence in Ukraine - Rebellion Research

[306] Tristan Greene. Ukraine has become the world's testing ground for military robots. *Thenextweb.com*. 21 December 2022. Ukraine has become the world's testing ground for military robots (thenextweb.com)

[307] Elias Kruger. Warfare AI in Ukraine: How Algorithms are Changing Combat. *AI Theology*. 8 March 2022.

[308] Op. Cit. Greene. Ukraine has become the world's testing ground…

[309] Giulia Carbonaro. Russia's Colossal Tank Losses in Ukraine Are Due to This Fatal Flaw. *Newsweek*. 28 May 2022. Russia's Colossal Tank Losses in Ukraine Are Due to This Fatal Design Flaw (newsweek.com)

percentage of the precision ammunition available in stocks before the war.[310] [311] [312]

Ukraine had a large inventory of old and outdated Soviet military equipment. The Ukrainian military captured a large number of Russian military equipment abandoned as they retreated in the first three months of the war. Ukraine used modernized conventional weapons to defeat the Russian invaders, some retrofitted with AI. For example, 28 old Slovenian M-55S tanks dating from the 1950s upgraded with new technology were sent to Ukraine. The tanks were upgraded by the Israeli company STO RAVNE. They were upgraded with British L7 105-millimeter main guns to replace the old Soviet 100-millimeter guns. The new guns use modern ammunition, including armor-piercing sabot rounds that can defeat the Russian T-72 tanks. The new guns have modern fire-control computer-driven systems while moving. The tanks were upgraded with a laser-warning system to alert the crew and deploy smoke grenades when an anti-tank missile is incoming. They had reactive armor installed, an original Israeli invention. To top it all, the old engines were replaced with new 600 horsepower engines.[313] Ukrainian tanks and crews performed better than the Russian tanks.

Ukraine had a considerable number of FIM-92 Stinger missiles. These are man-portable air defense weapons manufactured in the U.S., that function as infrared-homing surface-to-air missiles. It can be fired from helicopters as an air-to-air Stinger or from multiple types of ground vehicles. They have been around since early 1981. The Ukrainian military had been supplied with FGM-148 Javelin advanced anti-tank missiles, which have been around since the mid-1990s. It uses fire-and-forget automatic infrared guidance to reach its target.[314] They were equipped with British-manufactured Starstreak short-range surface-to-air high-velocity missiles or MANPADS. This weapon has been around since the late 1990s. Based on published reports, Russian helicopter pilots fear this weapon for its effectiveness.[315] It was used to shoot down multiple Russian

---

[310] ERR, News. EDF intelligence chief: Russia still has long-term offensive capabilities. 9 December 2022. EDF intelligence chief: Russia still has long-term offensive capabilities | News | ERR

[311] Daily Mail. Ukrainian forces destroy Russian T-73 in tank duel: Armoured vehicle explodes in a fireball after going head-to-head with mechanised brigade. *Daily Mail*. 12 December 2022. Ukrainian forces destroy Russian T-73 in tank duel | Daily Mail Online

[312] Yaron Steinbuch. Russia reportedly loses most advanced tank during fighting in Ukraine. *New York Post*. 5 May 2022. Russia reportedly loses most advanced tank in Ukraine (nypost.com)

[313] David Axe. Slovenia Is Giving Ukraine Some Very Old Tanks. But Age Can Be Deceiving. *Forbes*. Slovenia Is Giving Ukraine Some Very Old Tanks. But Age Can Be Deceiving. (forbes.com)

[314] The Ukrainians have been very successful using the FGM-148 Javelin portable surface-to-air missiles to blowup Russian tanks and armored vehicles. (See Jack Buckby. New Footage Shows Javelin Missile Hitting Russian Armor in Ukraine. MSN. 25 February 2023. New Footage Shows Javelin Missile Hitting Russian Armor in Ukraine (msn.com)

[315] See video: The Starstreak Missile that Russian helicopter pilots Fear the most - YouTube

helicopters.[316] In the use of conventional weapons, the Ukrainian military performed much better than the Russian military.

As the war continued, NATO members stepped up the delivery of military equipment to Ukraine. For example, in January 2023, France pledged to deliver light tanks to Ukraine. The French-built AMX-10 tanks were designed to move fast and exploit battlefield breakthroughs. Ukraine continued to beg for more main battle tanks, including the French-made Leclerc, the German Leopard 2, and the U.S. Abrams.[317] At about the same time, the U.S. confirmed that several dozen Bradley medium-armored combat vehicles were being sent to Ukraine as part of a $2.85 billion aid package.[318] [319] Finally, the U.S. and Germany agreed to provide main battle tanks to Ukraine, but they may not arrive until the Spring or Summer of 2023.

---

[316] Sabrina Johnson. UK missile 'shoots down Russian helicopter in Ukraine. *Metro.co.uk*. 2 April 2022. UK Starstreak missile 'shoots down Russian helicopter in Ukraine' | Metro News

[317] MSN.Com. Western tanks seen key to Ukraine battlefield breakthrough. *AFP*. 5 January 2023. Western tanks seen key to Ukraine battlefield breakthrough (msn.com)

[318] Lolita Baldor and Matthew Lee. US to send Ukraine dozens of Bradleys in $2.85B aid package. *Associated Press*. 5 January 2023. US to send Ukraine dozens of Bradleys in $2.85B aid package | AP News

[319] Andreas Rinke and Susan Heavey. Germany and U.S. agree to send combat vehicles to Ukraine. *Reuters*. 5 January 2023. Germany and U.S. agree to send combat vehicles to Ukraine | Reuters

ESTIMATE OF RUSSIAN LOSSES
[320] [321] [322] [323] [324] [325] [326]
As of 23 June 2023

	Before the war	Lost in the war
Troops	~850,000+ ~250,000 reservists	~223,910 killed ~284,280 injured (low estimate)
Tanks	~ 2,700+ as many as 9,000 old tanks, most of them in disrepair, including about 400 T-54 and T-55 tanks manufactured in the late 1940s after WWII	~4024 (Including old tanks brought back to service)
Armored Vehicles	~30,000	~7,804
Artillery systems		~4015 (Artillery fire reduced by as much as 75%, and using artillery shells as old as 40 years – ammunition supply a big problem due to poor logistics) - At least 619 Multiple Launch Rocket Systems and 383 anti-aircraft batteries have been taken out of action
UAVs – operational and tactical	~1707	~ 3,460
Aircraft	~4,000	~ 314 fix-wing airplanes ~ 308 helicopters
Cruise missiles	unknown	~ 1,222
Mercenaries Wagner Group	Unknown ~38,244	~ 30,000
Naval ships		~18
Multiple-launch rocket systems	Unknown	~559
Trucks	Unknown	~ 6,731 trucks of all kinds, including fuel trucks
Specialty vehicles	Unknown	~ 548

---

[320] David Brennan. Russia Loses 24 Tanks in a Day as 100,000 Death Toll Nears: Ukraine. *Newsweek*. 12 December 2022. Russia Loses 24 Tanks in a Day As 100,000 Death Toll Nears: Ukraine (newsweek.com)

[321] UAWAR.NET. 26 December 2022. Russia-Ukraine War 2022: Statistics and Facts | UAwar

[322] Natasha Bertrand, Oren Liebermann, Alex Marquardt. Russian artillery fire down nearly 75%, US officials say, in the latest sign of struggles for Moscow. CNN. 10 January 2023. Russian artillery fire down by nearly 75%, US officials say, in latest sign of struggles for Moscow | CNN Politics

[323] Ukrainska Pravda. Ukrainian defenders kill about 500 Russian soldiers and destroy 11 armored combat vehicles and 6 UAVs in one day. 18 April 2023. Ukrainian defenders kill about 500 Russian soldiers and destroy 11 armored combat vehicles and 6 UAVs in one day (msn.com)

[324] Ukrainska Pravda. Ukrainian forces kill 640 Russian invaders, destroy 4 tanks and 3 UAVs over 24 hours. Ukrainska Pravda. 26 April 2023. Ukrainian forces kill 640 Russian invaders, destroy 4 tanks and 3 UAVS over 24 hours (msn.com)

[325] Ukrainska Pravda. Ukrainian defenders kill 750 Russian soldiers in one day. Ukrainska Pravda. 12 May 2023. Ukrainian defenders kill 750 Russian soldiers in one day (msn.com)

[326] Ukrainska Pravda. Ukraine's Armed Forces destroy 12 Russian tanks and 22 artillery systems in one day. 17 June 2023. Ukraine's Armed Forces destroy 12 Russian tanks and 22 artillery systems in one day (msn.com)

Ukrainian Weaponized AI

Ukraine managed to contain the Russian invasion in part through the use of AI tools of modern warfare. Lots of weaponized commercially available equipment has been used for the war effort by using enhanced AI technology. Ukraine additionally exploited information readily available on the Internet to support its defense systems (The drawback is that the information is not always accurate.)[327] For example, Ukraine used advanced social media tools to undermine the morale of Russian military forces.[328] A case in point, using biometrics, including facial recognition powered by IA, Ukraine can identify dead Russian soldiers and notify their relatives, thus undermining popular support for President Vladimir Putin's war.

General Valerii Zaluzhbyi
Commander-in-Chief
Ukrainian Armed Forces

Ukraine is using AI-powered biometrics to identify Russian criminals who have committed atrocities against Ukrainian soldiers and civilians. Using AI, the Ukrainian military has been able to identify voice patterns of Russian commanders to identify their movements and plans. Conceivably, they could also issue false commands to Russian troops. Could they mimic the voice of General Gerasimov and issue commands to confuse Russian lower-level officers? Unmanned aerial vehicles (UAVs) enhanced with AI tools are used to recognize and attack specific Russian military targets.[329] [330]

AI weapons were imported by Ukraine from the Baltic States, Great Britain, Poland, Sweden, and the U.S. Among them are:

- **Bayraktar TB2** - A Turkish medium-altitude long-endurance UAV manufactured by Baykar Makina Sanayi ve Ticaret A.S., that can be used in combat. It can be adapted to carry laser-guided smart munition, such as the TBs gliding missile, which can pierce a 200 mm RHA steel or medium hardness. It has a range of 150 kn.

---

[327] General Sir Jim Hockenhull (UK Commander of the Strategic Command). How open-source intelligence has shaped the Russia-Ukraine war. 9 December 2022. How open-source intelligence has shaped the Russia-Ukraine war - GOV.UK (www.gov.uk)

[328] Ashish Dangwal. Ukraine Uses 'Controversial' Artificial Intelligence Tech In Its War Against Russia As Kiev Looks to Win the 'Digital War." *The Eurasian Times*. 7 April 2022.

[329] @Mobidev. Artificial Intelligence & Modern Wars: How Ukrainian Cyber Defense & DIIA Leverage AI to Fight Back. 9 May 2022. Artificial Intelligence & Modern Wars: How Ukrainian Cyber Defense & DIIA Leverage AI to Fight Back | HackerNoon

[330] Pavlo Kryvenko. "Artificial Intelligence" in the Russian-Ukrainian war. *NewGeopolitics.org*. 13 June 2022. "Artificial Intelligence" in the Russian-Ukrainian war - New Geopolitics Research Network

- **Switchblade** – This U.S.-manufactured high-precision strike, backpackable, tube-launched miniature loitering munitions has intelligence, surveillance, and reconnaissance (ISR) capabilities. There are two variants, the Switchblade 300 and the Switchblade 600. These systems were introduced around 2011. The U.S. agreed to supply these AI-equipped systems to Ukraine, but it is not clear when they arrived and were first used in combat. These missiles allow warfighters to fly, track, and strike non-line-of-sight targets and light-armored vehicles.[331]

- **THeMIS UGVs** – Manufactured in Germany by Milrem – Germany's Ministry of Defense ordered at least 14 of these vehicles to be sent to Ukraine – These are unarmed vehicles for demining operations and for the evacuation of casualties. However, it could also be used as an autonomous weapon to carry explosives to targets. The contract to deliver these weapons to Ukraine was signed on 29 November 2022. Seven of the robots will be configured for casualty evacuation. The first units were expected to be delivered in December 2022, and the rest by April 2023. These systems are used by several NATO members, including Estonia, France, Germany, Netherlands, Norway, Spain, the UK, and the U.S.[332]

Ukraine received other types of advanced weapons, not necessarily tied to AI, that provide them with advanced warfighting capabilities.[333] For example, the Ground Launched Small Diameter Bomb (GLSDB), which has a greater reach than other rockets, including the American-supplied High Mobility Artillery Rocket System (HIMARS). The HIMARS has a reach of about 48 miles. The GLDDB has a reach of about 94 miles and will be able to target Russian supply lines in their rear formations. These rockets will force the Russians to store ammunition storage and resupply sites further back behind their front lines.[334]

Ukrainian AI developers invented, manufactured, and deployed advanced weapons systems, among them:

- **Kamikaze drone ST-35 "Thunder"** – This Ukrainian-built weapons system is described as a "loitering munition," and as an unmanned aircraft system. This system has been around since 2019 and was designed and built for the Ukrainian military. It has a ground control station, optical payload, warhead,

---

[331] *Army Technology*. 8 April 2022. Switchblade® Tactical Missile System - Army Technology (army-technology.com)

[332] *European Security & Defence*. THeMIS UGVs for Ukraine (euro-sd.com)

[333] Note that these weapons are guided by GPS systems, which guide the rockets deep into enemy lines. They are manufactured jointly by Boeing Co. and the Swedish SAAB AM.

[334] Mike Stone and Max Hunder. Ukraine's new weapon will force a Russian shit. *Reuters*. 3 February 2023. Ukraine's new weapon will force a Russian shift (msn.com)

multi-rotor, dropping module, relay module, and antenna complex. It can be adapted with multiple types of warheads, including anti-tank explosives.[335]

- **Attack UAV helicopter RZ-500** – This Ukrainian-designed and built UAV attack helicopter system was introduced at some point in 2021. It can fly for up to three hours and has a maximum range of about 300 km, with a tactical radius of 60 to 80 km.  It can fly at low altitudes and be invisible to enemy radar. The missile has a range of up to 7.5 km.[336] [337]

- **People's Drone PD-1 / PD-2** – The Ukrainian-designed and manufactured PD-1 is an unmanned aerial system (UAS) that was introduced around 2016. It can be equipped with a variety of payloads for different missions. It can be flown in either pilot-assisted or fully autonomous modes and can fly missions for up to 10 hours. It is manufactured by  UkrSpecSystems.[338] The PD-2 ISR was approved for military operations in 2020 by the Ukrainian military. The VTOL configuration does not need a runway and can take off and land anywhere can operate in extreme weather conditions, and is difficult to detect and track. It is equipped with anti-jamming capabilities.[339]

- **RZ-500 attack drone** – This Ukrainian missile-armed designed and manufactured unmanned combat rotorcraft was introduced in 2021. It can fly for up to two hours and has a range of about 186 miles.[340]

- **ST-35 Silent Thunder loitering munition drone** – This Ukrainian-designed and built UAV loitering munition system was designed as a precision-guided weapon system and was introduced in 2019. It is guided semi-automatically.

---

[335] Army Technology. ST-35 Silent Thunder Loitering Munitions, Ukraine. Army Technology. 2 March 2022. ST-35 Silent Thunder Loitering Munition, Ukraine (army-technology.com)

[336] *Global Security*. Ramzay RZ-500. GlobalSecurity.org. Ramzay RZ-500 (globalsecurity.org)

[337] Staff writer. Ukraine Unveils Unmanned Combat Rotorcraft. *The Defense Post.* 23 June 2021. Ukraine Unveils Unmanned Combat Rotorcraft (thedefensepost.com)

[338] Air Force Technology. PD-1 Unmanned Aerial System. 4 April 2017. PD-1 Unmanned Aerial System (UAS), Ukraine (airforce-technology.com)

[339] Army Technology. PD-2 Unmanned Aerial System, Ukraine. Army Technology. 17 November 2021. PD-2 Unmanned Aerial System, Ukraine (army-technology.com)

[340] Staff Writer. Ukraine Unveils Unmanned Combat Rotorcraft. *The Defense Post.* 23 June 2021. Ukraine Unveils Unmanned Combat Rotorcraft (thedefensepost.com)

It employs a human operator to locate targets but can perform an autonomous flight, and can dive at a target autonomously. It can be equipped with different types of warheads, including anti-tank high-explosives. It can fly for about one hour.[341]

- **Hunter RSVK-M2 Unmanned Ground Vehicles** – This Ukrainian 6x6 robotic unmanned ground vehicle (UGV) can perform multiple roles in combat and can be armed with multiple weapons. [342] This UGV has been around since 2015. There is very little information available on open source about how these systems have been used to combat Russian invaders in 2022.[343] [344]

- **Anti-aircraft missile system Stugna-P** – This Ukrainian-designed and manufactured man-portable anti-tank guided missile was adopted by the Ukrainian military as far back as 2011. It is heavy and needs three operators. These systems weigh as much as 92.5 kg, making them difficult to handle. It has a range of about five km. It has been widely used against Russian tanks in the war. It is known to have destroyed T-72B3, T-89U, T80BVM, and T-90 tanks.[345]

Ukraine's AI Companies

AI is on the frontlines of the defensive war in Ukraine.[346] Long before the Russian invasion, Ukrainian IT specialists had made significant advances in AI and gained a well-established global presence. The Ukrainian Government developed a strategy to expand research and development (R&D) on AI technology, in an unregulated environment. It has been estimated that as many as 150 Ukrainian companies were active in AI technology by 2020, making the

---

[341] Army Technology. ST-35 Silent Thunder Loitering Munitions, Ukraine. *Army Technology*. 2 March 2022. ST-35 Silent Thunder Loitering Munition, Ukraine (army-technology.com)

[342] Hunter RSVK-M2 Ukrainian 6x6 Unmanned Ground Vehicle (UGV). ODIN - OE Data Integration Network (army.mil)

[340] What happened to RSVK-M2 and Uran-9 UGV on Ukrainian battlefields? *Bulgarianmilitary.com*. 13 April 2022. What happened to RSVK-M2 & Uran-9 on Ukrainian battlefields? (bulgarianmilitary.com)

[344] Sylan Malyasov. Ukraine is field testing its new combat drone in the Donbass region. *Defense-blog.com*. 4 May 2020. Ukraine is field testing its new combat drone in the Donbass region (defence-blog.com)

[345] Stugna-P anti-tank guided missile. Stugna-P Anti-Tank Guided Missile | Military-Today.com

[346] Jeremy Kahn. A.I. is on the front lines of the war in Ukraine. *Fortune*. 1 March 2021. A.I. goes to war in Ukraine | Fortune

country the leader in Eastern Europe.[347] [348] Based on multiple articles published since 2019, Kyiv had emerged as one of the top locations for AI startup companies not only in Europe but globally.[349] Historically, wars have stimulated R&D and resulted in significant inventions, and as part of this tradition, AI will advance as a result of the Russian invasion of Ukraine. Both sides will invest a lot of resources in the weaponization of AI. Ukraine has abundant young talent in AI, documented by published pictures of young prominent entrepreneurs and tech experts.

The Government of Ukraine established an *'Expert Committee on the Development of Artificial Intelligence,'* as part of the Ministry of Digital Transformation, in 2019.[350] By 2021, Ukraine's IT sector was expected to reach $10 billion in value, employing over 185,000 IT specialists.[351] It was tasked with increasing Ukraine's competitiveness in AI. Vitaliy Goncharuk was named Head of the Committee.[352] Ukrainians have been global leaders in AI development, including establishing companies all over the world. For example, Vitaliy Goncharuk established Augmented Pixels, Inc. in Palo Alto, California, in 2011. The company is linked to other companies using AI for machine learning, augmented reality, and autonomous navigation. He participated in numerous conferences in the U.S. related to AI, including sponsors like the National Academy of Sciences and NASA.

Vitaliy Goncharuk
Head of Ukraine's Expert Committee on AI Development

Ukrainian IT-AI companies cover many fields, including *Chatbots*, *Machine Learning*, *Natural Language Processing*, *Robotics*, and other key technology sectors. Among the top Ukrainian companies are *'Grammarly,'* which produces an advanced AI-powered writing assistant, which functions as an extension of Microsoft Office. *'Aitheon,'* a robotics innovator that uses AI to automate business operations. *'Traces.AI'* uses AI to support biometrics used by security cameras,

---

[347] Vitaliy Goncharuk. Ukraine's roadmap to an artificial intelligence future. Op. cit.

[348] Artificial Intelligence in Ukraine. Rebellionresearch.com. 17 March 2021. Artificial Intelligence in Ukraine - Rebellion Research

[349] Editorial team. 7 most prominent tech companies born in Ukraine. *Silicon Canals*. 18 June 2020. 7 most prominent tech companies born in Ukraine | Silicon Canals

[350] Експертний комітет з питань розвитку штучного інтелекту при Міністерстві цифрової трансформації

[351] There are 79 Companies in Ukraine that provide Artificial Intelligence Services! Top 10+ Artificial Intelligence Companies in Ukraine (2023) - TechBehemoths

[352] Expert Committee on the Development of Artificial Intelligence under the Ministry of Digital Transformation of Ukraine. The Expert Committee on Artificial Intelligence (en) (ai.org.ua)

currently in use to track people who test positive for COVID-19 using thermal imaging cameras. *'GitLab,'* helps IT companies to work together in security and ops teams, while increasing developer productivity, across 65 countries. The company has over 1,200 employees. *'Preply'* uses AI for machine learning, for example, teaching at least 50 languages online to thousands of students all over the world in just about every country. *'RefaceAI,'* uses AI for *'face-swapping,'* a technology used in the entertainment industry, including keeping emotions, skin colors, and other features of the faces being swapped. *'People.ai,'* uses AI to help sales staff to work more efficiently with customers, improving marketing programs. One of the most interesting aspects of these Ukrainian companies is that they are staffed by very young people, as witnessed by published pictures of the entrepreneurs and top technical staff.[353]

One example of the creativity of Ukrainian technology companies is the development of an anti-drone gun to intercept and down Russian drones (UAVs) to neutralize and capture them intact to obtain intelligence from them. The inventor and manufacturer is the Ukrainian company Kvertus Technology, and the weapon is called 'KVS G-6,' with a range of about 1.8 miles.[354]

Ukraine's IT Army

As soon as Ukrainian IT experts heard that Russia had invaded their country on 24 February 2022, a call went out on Facebook to recruit volunteers to create a cyber army to defend their country. It did not take very long for as many as 1000 Ukrainian cybersecurity experts to volunteer their services. In coordination with the Ministry of Defense and the National Security and Defense Council, they organized themselves to fight a cyberwar.[355]

There are too many Ukrainian companies in AI to list them all, but this is a fairly complete list:

---

[353] Editorial team. 7 most prominent tech companies born in Ukraine. Op. Cit.

[354] Alia Shoaib. How Ukraine uses high-tech anti-drone guns to down Russian drones and recover intelligence from them. MSN. How Ukraine uses high-tech anti-drone guns to down Russian drones and recover intelligence from them (msn.com)

[355] Jyoti Mann. I helped create a 'cyber army' to help Ukraine defeat Russia. We can't fight with guns, but we can fight with our laptops. MSN. 18 February 2023. I helped create a 'cyber army' to help Ukraine defeat Russia. We can't fight with guns, but we can fight with our laptops. (msn.com)

UKRAINIAN ARTIFICIAL INTELLIGENCE COMPANIES (Sample)

20 Thousand Leagues	Fortifier	Relevant Software
Abto Software	Giant Leap Lab	Requestum
Academy Smart	GitLab	Rinf.tech
Acropolium	Go Wombat	Rocket Harbor
Aitheon	Honeycomb Software	S-PRO
Agiliway	HumanIT	Sannacode
Apriorit	Idealogic	Scalamandra
Archer Software	Inoxoft	Singularika
Arsmoon	INSERT	Sloboda Studio
Best Business-Out-Of-Business	Intellect	Softgroup
	Integrio Systems	Softjourn
Business-Automatics-JSC	Intent Solutions Group	Solvve
Chatbots	ITRex Group	SourceX
CHI Software	Jappware	SPD
Clover Dynamics	Jazzros	Symphony Solutions
DarkLime	JetSoftPro	Tallium Inc.
Data Pro Software Solutions	Lemberg Solutions	Team Harbor
	Litslink	Techprostudio
Data Science UA	Lucid Reality Labs	Temy
DataRoots Labs	MadAppGang	The APP Solutions
DB2 Limited	Magnise	Traces.AI
Developex	Optimum-web	TrendLine Global
Devrain	People.ai	Uinno
EAvergreen	Postindustria	WebbyLab
Edvantis	Preply	Webdevelop PRO
Embrox Solutions	Proffiz	Yellow
Empat	Prostir	Yotalabs
Exadel	Quantum	Zfort Group
Flyaps	RefaceAI	

Multiple sources were used to compile the list[356] [357] [358] [359] [360]

---

[356] Top Artificial Intelligence Companies in Ukraine. Clutch. Top Artificial Intelligence Companies in Ukraine - 2023 Reviews | Clutch.co

[357] Editorial team. 7 most prominent tech companies born in Ukraine. Op. Cit.

[358] Tech Behemoths. There are 79 Companies in Ukraine that provide Artificial Intelligence Services. Top 10+ Artificial Intelligence Companies in Ukraine (2023) - TechBehemoths

[359] GoodFirm. Top Artificial Intelligence companies in Ukraine. 2 January 2023. Top Artificial Intelligence Companies in Ukraine 2023 | GoodFirms

[360] 100 Artificial Intelligence (AI) Companies in Ukraine. Updated January 2023. 100 Artificial Intelligence (AI) Companies in Ukraine (topdesignfirms.com)

Russian Weaponized AI

As previously mentioned, President Putin in 2018, launched a national AI development program, as part of the so-called *'Digital Economy Program.'* (*Программа «Цифровая экономика»*) The focus of the program was: information infrastructure, information security, digitalization of public services, end-to-end digital technologies, human capital, and adaptation of the regulatory environment.[361] Contrary to the situation in Ukraine, the AI sector in Russia is dominated by state-owned companies, which significantly reduces the level of freedom and creativity for IT specialists. The principal AI entities in Russia are *Gazprom Neft*, the country's fourth largest oil company; *Rostec*, a state-owned company involved primarily in the development of weaponized AI systems, and which naturally, operates in secrecy; *Skolkovo Foundation*, a key entity for funding and hosting technology start-ups, including funneling young people, including university students into hi-tech areas, and funding R&D into such areas as AI; and *Yandex*, Russia's largest and most successful privately-owned technology company. At one point, it had a relationship with Sberbank, which fell apart.[362]

Relations with foreign hi-tech companies are limited, but a rare exception was the establishment of the South Korean company Samsung, which established the so-called Samsung Research and Development Center in Moscow in 1992, which was further expanded in 2018. Russia maintains relations with some American academic institutions, for example, the Massachusetts Institute of Technology (MIT.) Despite government controls and a tendency for the state to control every aspect of the Russian economy, there are possibly as many as about 200 small private companies involved in the development of AI technologies. There is limited information in the open domain about what these companies focus on, and whatever is available may be tainted with disinformation. It is doubtful that the Russian Government would allow private companies to be involved in substantial research to weaponize AI. However, the Russian Government may have used these companies as 'fronts' to obtain Western technology by circumventing American export controls.

Russia started incorporating weaponized AI systems right from the start of the war in February 2022, particularly as it became evident that the Ukrainians were not going to surrender, and in fact, defeated Russian conventional weapons and military formations in the first 30 days of the invasion. The Russian military used hackers with AI-powered system tools to disrupt Ukraine's communication systems and disrupt utilities, including knocking out satellites that serviced not only Ukraine but also multiple European countries that suffered collateral damage. NATO countries

---

[361] Lee Sullivan. Artificial Intelligence in Russia. *Geohistory.today*. Artificial Intelligence in Russia geohistory.today)

[362] Ibid.

counteracted Russian actions by providing technology to mitigate Russian attacks and build formidable cyber defenses.³⁶³

Russians systematically use technology illegally obtained from the U.S. and other NATO countries to defeat Ukrainian weaponized AI. The Russians obtained and used technology from AutoCAD, IBM, Cisco, Cloudflare, Google, Microsoft, Oracle, and other companies in their weaponized AI. ³⁶⁴ Strong sanctions are long overdue against companies that put ethics in a second plane to increase profits. Access to Western commercial satellites, advanced communications and, GIS systems enables the Russian military to successfully target critical Ukrainian infrastructure and military targets.

Russian air-to-air missile R-37M
Source: *Pravda.ru 11 Jan. 2023*

Российские солдаты идут в бой против Украины с небольшим количеством еды, несколькими пулями и инструкциями, взятыми из Википедии за оружие, которым они едва умеют пользоваться...

Russian soldiers go into battle against Ukraine with little food, few bullets and instruction grabbed from Wikipedia for weapons they barely know how to use...

---

³⁶³ The war in Ukraine is exposing the limits of cyber warfare- and Russian hackers. 24 November 2022. The Ukraine conflict has exposed the limits of cyber warfare (thenextweb.com)

³⁶⁴ Anastassia Fedyk. Commentary: Russia is using Western technology in the war against Ukraine. Here's how to stop it. *Yakima Herald-Republic.* 25 December 2022. Commentary: Russia is using Western technology in the war against Ukraine. Here's how to stop it | Opinion | yakimaherald.com

Russian Hi-Tech Weapons Systems

Russia has used weapons systems with advanced technology, although it could be a stretch to denominate them *'weaponized AI.'* For example, Russia has used its hypersonic Kinzhal (Dagger)missiles against Ukraine, with some success, but they have been shot down by American Patriot anti-missile defense systems. However, when they were used in a missile attack against Ukraine, they were not shot down, because the Ukrainians did not have an operational Patriot system. These highly maneuverable missiles were probably launched from MIG-31s. The Russians launched at least 81 missiles against Ukrainian targets, including at least six Kinzhal (28 Kh-101) or Kh-555 hypersonic missiles, together with Kalbr sea-launched cruise missiles, and Kh-22 anti-ship cruise missiles, Kh-59 guided surface-to-air missiles and Kh-31 anti-ship missiles against ground targets.[365] [366] [367]

---

[365] Nick Mordowanec. Russia's Kinzhal Missiles Can Be Shot Down By This Weapon, Ukraine Reveals. Newsweek.9 March 2023. Russia's Kinzhal Missiles Can Be Shot Down By This Weapon, Ukraine Reveals (msn.com)

[366] Hanna Arhirova and Elena Becatoros. Russian missile barrage slams into Ukrainian cities; 6 dead, AP News. 9 March 2023. Russian missile barrage slams into Ukrainian cities; 6 dead | AP News

[367] BBC, Ukraine war: Russia fires hypersonic missiles in new barrage. BBC. 9 March 2023. Ukraine war: Russia fires hypersonic missiles in new barrage - BBC News

Russian Military Sloppiness

> **Common sense** *is sound and prudent judgment based on a simple perception of the situation or facts.*
>
> *Merriam-Webster Dictionary*

AI is not an antidote for a lack of *'common sense,'* poor judgment, carelessness, incompetence, or sloppiness. During 2022, it became increasingly self-evident, that the Russian military establishment's performance in its war against Ukraine was very sloppy. A former Russian military commander, Igor Girkin, pointed out the considerable mishandling of just about everything associated with the conflict.[368] The troops were not motivated and disliked their commanders. Within days of the start of the war, Russia had lost an estimated $5 billion in military hardware (tanks, armored vehicles, artillery, aircraft, and helicopters.) Ukrainian defenders captured Russian weapons of all types, including large caches of ammunition, and turned them around against their former owners. It turned out that Russian military equipment was poorly designed, ineffective in combat, and easily defeated using NATO member weapons. Another serious problem was that Russian advanced military equipment was found to have Western, particularly, American technology. *It became very clear that Russia was dependent on American technology for its advanced weapons systems!* [369] How did the Russians evade U.S. export controls? Either they are very clever, or American law enforcement, customs, and intelligence personnel are very lazy, stupid, or do not understand the importance of the tasks assigned to them.[370]

On 2 January 2023, Russia acknowledged heavy casualties in one of Ukraine's deadliest strikes. Based on press reports, Russian commanders stored

---

[368] Andrew Stanton. Ex-Russian Commander Credits Ukraine's Success to Kremlin's Sloppiness. *Newsweek*. 1 January 2023. Ex-Russian Commander Credits Ukraine's Success to Kremlin's Sloppiness (msn.com)

[369] Peter Suciu. Putin's Nightmare: Russia's Biggest Weapons Flops in Ukraine. Putin's Nightmare: Russia's 5 Biggest Weapons Flops in Ukraine (msn.com)

[370] This author encountered many examples of American unauthorized satellite technology banned from export while posted at the U.S. Embassy in Mexico, but not as part of his assigned work. Mexican consumers all over their country set up satellite antennas, receivers, descramblers, and related equipment to download American television. The author found that U.S. Customs focuses on checking imports, but does not pay the same attention to controlling exports, and in many cases could not tell a satellite receiver and descrambler from music equipment. The same chips used by these systems were used by NSA, which unsuccessfully tried to control their export. Technology exhibitions, endorsed by the U.S. Department of Commerce, included American companies exhibiting and selling banned items from export! He even took the U.S. Customs Attaché at the American Embassy in Mexico to one of these trade shows to point out what was going on. When the exhibitors flew back to the U.S. through the Dallas Airport after the show, they had a nasty surprise.

ammunition next to a large building that previously housed a vocational college in Makiivka, next to the regional capital of Donetsk. Using American-made HIMARS launchers Ukraine hit the barracks killing as many as 400 Russian soldiers, and wounding another 300. Russian only claimed that 63 of its troops were killed and a large number wounded. Russian sloppiness once again resulted in a heavy toll. How could Russian commanders decide to store ammunition next to barracks? As the ammunition exploded, it compounded the effect of the Ukrainian missile strike on the facility with secondary explosions.³⁷¹

One of the interesting stories behind the successful attack against the Russian military barracks in Makiivka is related to the use of not-that-sophisticated telecommunications equipment to detect the presence of cell phones. The Russian commanders allowed their troops to carry with them their cell phones, which they use to communicate with their families. The location of the cell phones, particularly the location from where numerous calls originate gives a signal to the Ukrainian intelligence assets of where a significant target is located. The Russians have made this stupid mistake over and over again, clearly showing a lack of discipline and incompetence.³⁷² All the AI in the world cannot help Russia if they lack basic common sense.³⁷³

Chief of the General Staff Of Russian Armed Forces Gen. Valery Gerasimov

As the Russian troops were getting slaughtered in Makiivka, Russian Minister of Defense, General Sergei Shoigu was videotaped at a New Year's party.³⁷⁴ The 51-second video was shared on Twitter and Telegram channels. Shoigu dancing and singing in a crowd of people... Lack of basic common sense starts at the top of the Russian chain of command. Indicative of the serious problems affecting the Russian military campaign, was the action taken by President Vladimir Putin on 12 January 2023, to name his top general, Valery Gerasimov (Валерий Васильевич Герасимов to take direct command of the war

---

³⁷¹ Reuters. Anger in Russia as scores of troops killed in one of war's deadliest strikes. *Reuters*. 2 January 2022. Anger in Russia as scores of troops killed in one of war's deadliest strikes | Reuters

³⁷² Brendan Cole. Russia Loses 10,000 Troops in Two Weeks: Ukraine. *Newsweek*.5 January 2023. Russia Loses 10,000 Troops in Two Weeks: Ukraine (msn.com)

³⁷³ TASS. Use of phones is cause of tragedy in Makeyevka – Russian Defense Ministry. *TASS Russian News Agency*. 3 January 2023. Use of phones is cause of tragedy in Makeyevka — Russian Defense Ministry - Military & Defense - TASS

³⁷⁴ Isabel Van Brugen. Fact Check: Did Russia's Shoigu Party as HIMARS decimated Makiivka Base? *Newsweek*. 4 January 2023. Fact Check: Did Russia's Shoigu Party as HIMARS Decimated Makiivka Base? (newsweek.com)

in Ukraine.[375] Since 2012, he served as Chief of the General Staff of the Russian Armed Forces, and the First Deputy Minister of Defense.

General Gerasimov graduated from the Kazan Higher Tank Command School, and moved up the ranks, serving as Chief of Staff of a tank regiment, and commander of the 144th Guards Motor Rifle Division in the Baltics. In 2014, he commanded the Russian forces that led to the annexation of Crimea. He may have been wounded in combat in Ukraine in May 2022. He was named to replace Sergey Surovikin as commander of Russian forces fighting in Ukraine. In December 2022, there were rumors that General Gerasimov had been fired by President Putin. Was the appointment to personally run the war a promotion or a demotion?[376]

Although credited with the so-called *'rejuvenation'* of the Russian military, recent mismanagement in Ukraine contradicts any notion that great improvements were made since General Gerasimov took over as Chief of Staff in 2012, and started promoting his *'new type of warfare,'* including weaponized AI, *'scientific modeling,'* dominance of the *'information space.'* Right after General Gerasimov reportedly took personal command of Russian troops in Ukraine, the Russian press reported that a Russian senior sergeant accidentally detonated a hand grenade in his dorm on Ukraine's border, killing 3 and injuring 16. All the AI in the world cannot overcome sloppiness and carelessness.[377] The Russian military leadership has turned out to be very dysfunctional, with one hand not knowing what the other one is doing.[378]

Not long after General Gerasimov took personal command of troops in Ukraine, another stupid accident was reported by the international press. The video became available of a Russian tank commander moving the turret of his tank around and accidentally sweeping off another tank at least five soldiers that were riding on top of an armored vehicle passing by.[379] All the AI technology in

---

[375] TASS. Gerasimov's appointment due to broader scope of objectives in Ukraine operation – Kremlin. 12 January 2023. Gerasimov's appointment due to broader scope of objectives in Ukraine operation — Kremlin - Military & Defense – TASS

[376] Alexander Ward, Matt Berg and Lawrence Ukenye. The good and bad of Gerasimov's 'promotion.' *Politico.* 12 January 2023. The good and bad of Gerasimov's 'promotion' – POLITICO

[377] Matthew Loh. A Russian senior sergeant accidentally detonated a hand grenade in his dorm on Ukraine's border, killing 3 and injuring 16. *Microsoft Business Insider.* 16 January 2023. A Russian sergeant accidentally detonated a hand grenade in his dorm on Ukraine's border, killing 3 and injuring 16 (msn.com)

[378] DNYUZ. To Fix Its Problems in Ukraine, Russia Turns to the Architect of the War. *DNTUZ.* 28 January 2023. To Fix Its Problems in Ukraine, Russia Turns to the Architect of the War – DNyuz

[379] Josh Milton. Blundering Russian tank commander takes out his own soldiers with his turret. Metro.co.UK. 2 February 2023. Blundering Russian tank commander takes out his soldiers with turret | Metro News

the world cannot replace basic common sense, and clumsy behavior, and prevent stupid accidents.

Despite placing General Gerasimov in direct command of troops participating in the invasion of Ukraine, and his strong background as a tank commander, as of the second week of February 2023, Russia continued to lose tanks and soldiers. According to an operational update on 7 February, the Russians lost at least 25 more tanks and had an estimated 1,900 soldiers killed in the previous two days. According to the Ukrainian military, Russia had already lost about 3,245 tanks since the start of the war. Ukrainians claimed to have captured at least 440 Russian main battle tanks, in addition to 659 armored vehicles.[380] It was also announced that a 10th Russian General, Major-General Dmitry Ulyanov, had been killed in Ukraine.[381]

Yevgeniy Prigozhin. Commander of Russian mercenary force Wagner Group, composed of convicted Russian criminals serving time in jail. They are offered freedom in exchange for fighting in Ukraine. The organization was created in 2014 and participated in the invasion of Crimea. They also participated in the civil war in Syria as part of Russian forces sent to support Syrian dictator Bashar al-Assad.

---

[380] Ellie Cook. Russia Loses 25 tanks in two days as video shows deadly strike. Ukraine. Newsweek. 7 February 2023. Russia Loses 25 Tanks in Two Days As Video Shows Deadly Strike: Ukraine (msn.com)

[381] Major-General Ulyanov was a previous commander of the elite 98th Guards Airborne Division, former Chief of Staff of the 7th Airborne Division, commander of the 1141st Artillery Regiment, and commander of the 98th Airborne Division. See: Tom Sanders. Another blow for Putin after the 10th senior commander killed fighting in Ukraine. MSN.Com. 7th February 2023. Another blow for Putin after 10th senior commander killed fighting in Ukraine (msn.com)

Russia Deploys Combat Robots to Fight Tanks

Right after the U.S. Germany, France, the UK, and other NATO members agreed to send about 321 tanks to Ukraine in advance of an expected Russian Spring offensive in 2023, the news media reported that Russia was deploying killer robots designed to destroy tanks. However, the Russian experience with these AI-powered military robots has not been good. They failed in Syria. The number of available robots is very limited, based on published reports.[382]

Тупой русский солдат
Dumb Russian soldier's jokes

---

[382] Matthew Impelli. Russia Deploys Combat Robots to Fight Tanks in Ukraine. *Newsweek.* 2 February 2023. Russia Deploys Combat Robots to Fight Tanks in Ukraine (msn.com)

RUSSIAN ARTIFICIAL INTELLIGENCE COMPANIES (Sample)
"Private" with government oversight Russian Style

AMAI	i-Neti	SkyGuru
Angels IT	Insilico Medicine	SoftMediaLab LLC
Antal Russia	Intspirit	Spirit DSP
Apri.group	ISS Art	Technaxis
Artezio	IT Test	Tieto
Atomic Creative	Iteora GmbH	TIQUM
BroutonLab	Iterative.ai	TraceAir
Burning Buttons LLC	LATECO	True engineering
Clever Data	LineUp	UVL Robotics
CodeInside	Mlvch	WayRay
CVisionLab	MobileUp	Webiomed
Dasha.ai	myTHE	Wollow
Digital Design	Napoleon IT	Working Geeks
Effective	Neurobotics	Xentaurs Engineering
ENBISYS	Ntechlab	Competence
ESTESIS Technologies	NTR Labs	Yandex
Everyone	Promobot LLC	ZeBrains
Exciting reality	QStudio.org	Zen
First Line Software	Roasted Ox Leg	Zenbot
Forest Valley	Roonyx	ZuZex
Geosplit	Rubius	ZYFR
Husky Jam	Simlabs Inc.	

Multiple sources were used to compile the list [383] [384] [385]

---

[383] Tech Behemoths. There are 17 companies in Russia that provide Artificial Intelligence Services! *Tech Behemoths*. Top 10+ Artificial Intelligence Companies in Russia (2023) – TechBehemoths

[384] GoodFirms. Top Artificial Intelligence companies in Russia. *GoodFirms*. 14 January 2023. Top Artificial Intelligence Companies in Russia 2023 | GoodFirms

[385] Golden. Artificial intelligence companies in Russia. *Golden*. Artificial intelligence companies in Russia | 216 results | Golden

Russian Air War Over Ukraine

The Russian air war over Ukraine has been characterized as an unexpected failure. Russia did not gain air superiority, despite considerable braggadocio about their AI. The principal fighter plane and ground support were provided by Su-30SM fighters, derived from the Soviet Sukhoi-27 planes (Flanker). Many of these planes were shot down by air defense systems, as well as by Ukraine pilots.[386] Over 70 Russian fighters were shot down in the first year of the war, a few more than the number of Ukrainian planes that were shot down. American AGM-88 HARM anti-radiation missiles were particularly effective against Russian planes.[387]

Russia's Su-75 Checkmate *(But the incorporated Russian AI technology was checkmated before it could take off...)*

This '5th-generation' stealth light tactical aircraft developed by Sukhoi aircraft for the Russian Aerospace Forces unveiled in 2021, seems to be another failure in the application of AI technology. To start with, it seems that the aircraft is dependent on imported semiconductors and high-tech machine tools, and has been rated a failure.[388] Based on published reports, it was built as a more advanced plane than the Su-7 and was conceived as a plane that could be exported. It was to have AI incorporated into an onboard computer and avionics system. However, there is no interest from potential foreign buyers. Challenges that plague this plane may not be resolved until the 2030s, and by then foreign competitors without a doubt would have developed more advanced fighter planes that would render the Su-75 a waste of money. Based on published reports, the Su-75 was to have an unmanned variant (CAV) using AI technology. In the Russian pipedreams, several countries, including Argentina, India, Vietnam, and several Arab and South American countries might have been interested in buying some of these aircraft, assuming they have the funds. The current assessment is as of January 2023, this plane is doomed.[389]

---

[386] Maya Carlin. Su-30SM: This Warplane Is the Backbone of the Russian Air Force in Ukraine. MSN. 6 March 2023. Su-30SM: This Warplane Is the Backbone of the Russian Air Force in Ukraine (msn.com)

[387] John Bacon. Ukraine has shot down 70 Russian jets; Russian protesters imprisoned for 'fake news': Live update. *USA Today*. 7 March 2023. Ukraine has shot down 70 Russian jets; Russian protester imprisoned for 'fake news': Live updates (msn.com)

[388] Peter Suciu. Russia's Su-75 Checkmate Stealth Fighter Is a Failure. *MSN*. 13 January 2023. Russia's Su-75 Checkmate Stealth Fighter Is A Failure (msn.com)

[389] Maya Carlin. Su-75: Russia's New Stealth Fighter Looks Doomed. *MSN*. 8 January 2023. Su-75: Russia's New Stealth Fighter Looks Doomed (msn.com)

Weaponizing AI: U.S. Experience

> *All is flux, nothing stays still.*
>
> Plato

Modern warfare is intrinsically tied to the development of *'autonomous weapons systems'* (AWS), and the weaponization of AI. Based on numerous published assessments, the U.S. is ahead in the development of AI technologies, including autonomous weapons systems. As of 2021, the U.S. was the global leader in investments in R&D related to AI, as well as the country with the largest number of experts on AI. The U.S. has been rated as the leader in eight of 17 indicators in emerging technologies, including AI. However, although the U.S. is the current leader, it does not mean that American civilian and military leaders, and the American public, understand the implications.[390] This is a very serious business. As other nations step up their R&D investments, competition is increasing, and leadership could be lost overnight. Nothing is forever. American technology is exported illegally, intellectual property is being stolen, and the quality of education is declining, making it increasingly possible that the U.S. could lose its preeminence in AI. *And then, what?*

2021 ARTIFICIAL INTELLIGENCE INDEX

Rank	Country	Index Score	Rank	Country	Index Score
1	USA	100	7	Finland	63.09
2	Singapore	67.22	8	Germany	63.09
3	Switzerland	67.14	9	Ireland	62.77
4	Netherlands	66.2	10	UK	62.05
5	Japan	64.22	11		
6	South Korea	64.11	20	PRC (China)	50.82
7	Sweden	64.05	n/a	Russia	n/a

Source: GlobalData / Investment Monitor
The US leads in R&D investment on AI, as well as talent. Economic and military competitiveness depends on investments in AI.
<u>Index shows US still leading world for AI - Investment Monitor</u>

According to MIT, of the top 13 AI leaders, seven are American companies. They are *Alphabet* (Google), *Enlitic*, *Facebook* (META), *IBM*, *Microsoft*, *Nvidia*, and *Tesla*.[391] The top ten countries assessed to be the leaders of AI are in alphabetical

---

[390] TARS. The Dangers of Military-Grade AI [Artificial Intelligence], SOBREP. 11 December 2021. <u>The Dangers of Military-Grade AI (Artificial Intelligence) | SOFREP</u>

[391] Lisa Calhoun. MIT Ranks the World's 13 Smartest Artificial Intelligence Companies – From chatbots to robots, these global leaders combine brains with business sense. *Inc.* 14 November 2016. <u>MIT Ranks the World's 13 Smartest Artificial Intelligence Companies | Inc.com</u>

order: China, France, Germany, India, Japan, Russia, Singapore, South Korea, Sweden, the UK, and the U.S. However, the National Security Commission on Artificial Intelligences has warned that the U.S. could lose its leadership in the next decade, as China and other countries continue to rapidly develop their capabilities.[392] To avoid losing leadership, action has been taken to enhance American competitiveness. The data and the assessments are contradictory. Not everyone agrees on the strategic and tactical value of autonomous weapons systems, and others raise ethical and moral questions about the technology.[393]

According to a study by the *Australian Strategic Policy Institute* (ASPI) quoted in a Reuters report on 2 March 2023, China has achieved a 'stunning lead' in 37 out of 44 critical and emerging technologies in defense, space, energy, and biotechnology. The Australian study was funded by the U.S. DOD. Although it is impossible to assess the accuracy of the finding from the outside, clearly it illustrates how serious the challenge is.[394] Nobody knows who is the '*top dog*,' because a lot of the action is kept in deep secrecy. Although the '*algorithmic warfare battlefield*' is not here yet, it is not far into the future.

Efforts to Maintain American Leadership in AI

On 12 October 2016, President Barack Obama issued two reports outlining plans and specific recommendations to maintain leadership in AI. The proposals listed the need to train the American workforce, improve American education, and aggressively recruit and attract immigrants with technology know-how in areas directly related to AI. It called for the government to focus investment on R&D in important areas in which private companies are not already investing. It suggested a review of regulations that may stand in the way of the development of AI, and create incentives for private sector investment in R&D. The two reports showed concern that the PRC has surpassed the U.S. in R&D and development of AI, and could emerge as a new global leader, dethroning the U.S.[395] [396] However, the reports defined AI as *a notional future AI system that*

---

[392] Liam Tung. Who leads the world on AI? A decade from now, it might not be the US. *ZDNet*. 2 March 2021. Who leads the world on AI? A decade from now, it might not be the US | ZDNET

[393] Amitai Etzioni and Oren Etzioni. Pros and Cons of Autonomous Weapons Systems. *Army University Press*. May-June 2017. Pros and Cons of Autonomous Weapons Systems (army.mil)

[394] Reuters. China holds 'stunning lead' over US in competition for key technology. *The Jerusalem Post*. 2 March 2023. China holds 'stunning lead' over US in competition for key technology (msn.com)

[395] Ajay Agraval, Joshua Gans, and Avi Goldfarb. The Obama Administration's Roadmap for AI Policy. *Harvard Business Review*. 21 December 2016. The Obama Administration's Roadmap for AI Policy (hbr.org)

[396] Ed Felten and Terah Lyons. The Administration's Report on the Future of Artificial Intelligence. 12 October 2016. The Administration's Report on the Future of Artificial Intelligence | whitehouse.gov (archives.gov)

exhibits intelligent behavior at least as advanced as a person across the full range of cognitive tasks." In other words, the reports were odd, and seemed to question the advances in AI, and the possibility of real machine learning and true artificial intelligence. There seemed to be more concern about the impact of AI on the well-being of low-wage, low-skilled workers, than on foreign enemies taking the lead in the weaponization of AI.

On 11 February 2019, President Donald J. Trump signed an *Executive Order on Maintaining American Leadership in Artificial Intelligence*. The purpose was to maintain the U.S. as the world leader in AI research and development (R&D) and stated that it is of paramount importance to maintaining economic and national security.[397] [398] In December 2020, President Trump signed another Executive Order, outlining principles for the U.S. Governments' use of AI. The principal concern was the need for the government to foster public trust and confidence in AI, and to protect privacy, civil rights, and civil liberties resulting from the development and use of AI.[399] No concerns were specifically mentioned about national security, foreign enemies developing weaponized AI, and taking the lead from the U.S.

On 25 August 2022, President Joe Biden signed an Executive Order to Implement the CHIPS and Science Act of 2022. This legislation responded to acute semiconductor shortages and aims at building a resilient semiconductor supply chain, expanding R&D, manufacturing, and infrastructure to improve the country's competitive edge on the world stage.

On 17 February 2023, the U.S. launched an initiative for the *'responsible'* use of weaponized AI, and autonomous weapons systems.[400] At a meeting in The Hague, the U.S. promoted an international effort to regulate or create some kind of *'order'* in the military use of AI, when historically, every nation at war has always rushed to create new and more advanced weapons to defeat their enemies. The only historically recognized responsible military doctrine is to defeat the enemy. The creation of autonomous weapons systems operating with

---

[397] Klint Finley. Obama Wants the Government to Help Develop AI: The President thinks it's time for the government to get more involved in artificial intelligence (up to a point). Wired. 12 October 2016. Obama Wants the Government to Help Develop AI | WIRED

[398] President Donald J. Trump. *Executive Order on Maintaining American Leadership in Artificial Intelligence.* 11 February 2019. Executive Order on Maintaining American Leadership in Artificial Intelligence – The White House (archives.gov)

[399] David Shepardson. Trump signs order on principles for U.S. government AI use. Reuters. 3 December 2020. Trump signs order on principles for U.S. government AI use | Reuters

[400] Mike Corder. US launches artificial intelligence military use initiative. Associated Press. 16 February 2023. US launches artificial intelligence military use initiative - ABC News (go.com)

Artificial Intelligence

AI making decisions without human intervention is a new phenomenon but without any evidence that as of April 2023, it has ever happened.

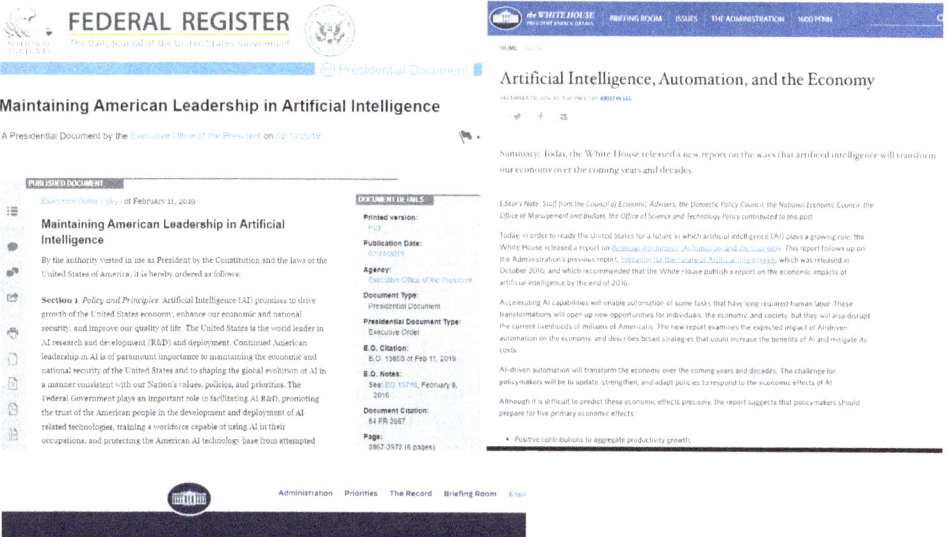

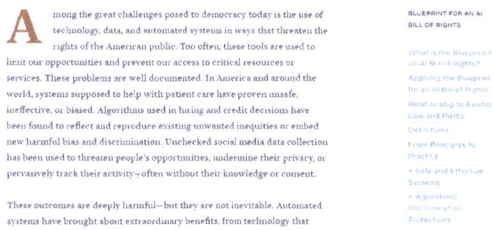

Education in the U.S. is in Crisis

> *All warfare is based on deception. There is no place where espionage is not used. Offer the enemy bait to lure him.*
>
> Sun Tzu

In addition to the incentive to transfer production overseas to lower costs, now there is another cause cited for going overseas. Unable to find quality employees at home, American tech companies are outsourcing technology jobs overseas. The U.S. is falling behind other countries in the quality of education, as witnessed by test scores. American students continue to rank lower than other countries in math and science assessments. The U.S. ranks 14th globally in the 25-34 age group with higher education (42%).[401] When an estimated 65 percent of Fourth Graders in the U.S. cannot read, it will be impossible to continue leading in global technology! [402] [403] [404]

As in other areas linked to AI, there are many contradictions in the question of education and the availability of talent necessary to maintain leadership. The U.S. is ranked as the top country with 'talent' related to AI technology and in the education of the workforce. There are an estimated 365,000 Chinese students attending school in American universities. Over one million Chinese students have completed advanced degrees in the U.S. since 2000, in science, technology, engineering, and mathematics, known as STEM area disciplines. [405] They go to the U.S. to get a top-quality education in technology areas. Why do they go to the U.S. instead of going to school in China, Russia, the UK, or anywhere else? That is a clear indication that the U.S. is perceived as the *'top dog.'* But what is the solution? In espionage these situations are a *'double edge sword,'* in the same way that China benefits from educating its people to go back to work for its military and intelligence organizations, the U.S. can also recruit Chinese students to return to their country to work as American spies. *'If you snooze, you lose!'* [406]

---

[401] Dr. Rabia Khan. United States is Falling Behind in Education, Data Reveals. *The Morning News.* 22 April 2021. United States Is Falling Behind in Education, Data Reveals - The Morning News

[402] The Free Press. Why 65 Percent of Fourth Graders Can't read. *The Free Press.* 11 February 2023. Why 65 Percent of Fourth Graders Can't Really Read (thefp.com)

[403] Kimberly Amadeo. U.S. Education Ranking Are Falling Behind the Rest of the World. *The Balance Money.* 13 April 2022. U.S. Education Rankings Are Falling Behind the Rest of the World (thebalancemoney.com)

[404] Pew Research Center. The US is falling behind academically. This is why. *World Economic Forum.* 22 February 2017. The US is falling behind academically. This is why | World Economic Forum (weforum.org)

[405] STEM is an acronym introduced by the U.S. National Science Foundation (NSF) in 2001.

[406] The Spanish proverb *'camarón que se duerme se lo lleva la corriente,'* translated as: *"a shrimp that falls asleep gets carried by the tide,"* may explain the dilemma somewhat better than *'If you snooze, you lose!'*

While other countries increase the number of young people attending college and going into science and technology careers, in the U.S. an increasing number of young people are opting out of college and going into alternative programs. For example, going into apprenticeship and vocational programs. College enrollment has declined by about 15 percent, while the number of young people going into apprenticeship programs has increased by more than 50 percent. The trend is not necessarily bad, as long as the number of young people go into such things as cybersecurity programs, but in the long term, a reduction in college students could be dangerous.[407]

Student Performance Across Subjects

Changes in average scores and scores at selected percentiles, by subject and grade

Subject	Grade	Current Year	Prior Year	Average score	Percentiles				
					10th	25th	50th	75th	90th
Mathematics	4	2022	2019	↓	↓	↓	↓	↓	↓
Mathematics	8	2022	2019	↓	↓	↓	↓	↓	↓
Reading	4	2022	2019	↓	↓	↓	↓	↓	◆
Reading	8	2022	2019	↓	↓	↓	↓	↓	↓

SHOW THE RESULTS FOR OTHER SUBJECTS

↑ Significant increase compared to last assessment year
◆ No significant difference compared to last assessment year
↓ Significant decrease compared to last assessment year

LATEST RELEASE

2022 Mathematics and Reading Report Cards at Grades 4 and 8

Compared to 2019 (before the pandemic):
- Average scores declined in both subjects and grades.
- Average scores declined for most states in both subjects and grades.
- Students' confidence in their mathematics and reading skills declined.

---

[407] Douglas Belkin. M o r e Students Are Turning Away from College Toward Apprenticeships. *Wall Street Journal*. 16 March 2023. More Students Are Turning Away from College and Toward Apprenticeships - WSJ

Shambolic American Export Controls[408]

> **If you do not change direction, you may end up where you are heading.**
>
> Lao Tzu

There are numerous examples of American and Western European semiconductors and hi-tech components used in Iranian weapons, including guided munitions and drones (UAVs) provided to Russia despite the export bans in place. Some of these components were manufactured since 2020, which indicates that this is a real and present challenge. Ukrainian technicians found components of Iranian weapons systems manufactured by more than 70 companies based in 13 different countries, and 82 percent of them were manufactured by companies based in the U.S. Some of these high-technology products had been manufactured in 2020 and 2021. They were found in the Shahed-131, Shahed-136, and Mohajer-6 UAVs. The Iranians have been able to circumvent American export controls.[409] [410] [411] Iranians have also been able to obtain Western technology for their R&D efforts to develop weapons of mass destruction (WMDs).[412]

Russia is circumventing American export controls, as witnessed by captured weapons systems in Ukraine. For example, Russian-modified Iranian UAVs were found to have chips made in the U.S. by Maxim and Microchip. Components manufactured by Altera USA, AMD, Texas Instruments, Linear Technology, and Rochester Electronics have been found in Russian advanced weapon systems. The same chips are used in many consumer products,

---

[408] Chaotic, disorganized, and mismanaged...

[409] Dissecting Iranian drones employed by Russia in Ukraine. Ukraine field dispatch. November 2022. Dissecting Iranian drones employed by Russia in Ukraine (arcgis.com)

[410] John Ismay. Iranian Weapons Built with Western Semiconductors Despite Sanctions. *The New York Times*. 22 November 2022. Iranian Weapons Built with Western Semiconductors Despite Sanctions - The New York Times (nytimes.com)

[411] Chris Livesay, Erin Lyall. Russia is bombarding Ukraine with drones guided by U.S.-made technology, and the chips are still flowing. CBS Evening News. 4 January 2023. Russia is bombarding Ukraine with drones guided by U.S.-made technology, and the chips are still flowing - CBS News

[412] Benjamin Weinthal. Iran sought nuclear weapons, technology for WMDs last year, reports find. *Fox News*. 3 May 2021. Iran sought nuclear weapons, and technology for WMDs last year, reports find | Fox News

including cars, smartphones, tablets, and appliances.[413] [414] Even in the middle of the Russian invasion of Ukraine, Russia can continue obtaining European and American technology, circumventing export controls.[415] Shockingly, Russian advanced weapons systems use AI packed with American components. These include a radar-equipped air defense command post vehicle, part of a Pantsir air defense system, a Ka-52 'Alligator' attack helicopter, and the AS-23A Kodiak cruise missile. The Russian Hypersonic Kinzhal missile is powered by American technology. Incredible, Russian high-precision weapons are packed with American technology![416] [417] [418]

Are Americans willfully blind to the consequences of acting stupid? Someone is messing up and screwing up in the enforcement of export controls. Albert Einstein is quoted as saying that to do the same thing over and over again but expecting a different result is the definition of insanity. What will it take to make corrections? Arrogance may be self-satisfying, but it can be very dangerous. Temper tantrums and embarrassment when it is found that high-tech products that are banned from export are components of weapons systems of unfriendly nations do not solve the problem. Gaslighting is not a solution to a very transcendental challenge.

---

[413] *Analog Devices*, a semiconductor manufacturer based in Massachusetts, bought out *Maxim Integrated Products Inc.* for $20.9 billion in 2020. *Maxim* manufactures mixed-signal integrated circuits for automotive, communications, and consumer products. *Microchip Technology Inc.* is headquartered in Chandler, Arizona, and manufactures semiconductors, memory cards, capacitors, integrated circuits, sensors, and other hi-tech products.

[414] Ian King. Analog Devices to Buy Rival Maxim in $21 Billion Chip Deal. *Bloomberg.* 13 July 2020. Analog Devices to Buy Rival Maxim in $21 Billion Chip Deal – Bloomberg

[415] Op. Cit. Chris Livesay, Erin Lyall, Russia is bombarding Ukraine…

[416] Tanmay Kadam. Made in USA! Russia's Most Advanced Weapons Are Shockingly Packed With 'American Components- Ukrainian Intelligence. *The Eurasian.* 29 May 2022. Made In USA! Russia's Most Advanced Weapons Are Shockingly Packed With 'American Components' -- Ukrainian Intelligence (eurasiantimes.com)

[417] Joe Saballa. US-Made Microchips Found in Captured Russian Weapons: Report. *The Defense Post.* 30 May 2022. US-Made Microchips Found in Captured Russian Weapons: Report (thedefensepost.com)

[418] Alex Hollings. Evidence Suggests Russia's 'Hypersonic' Kinzhal Missile is Powered by American Tech. Sandbox. 15 November 2022. Evidence suggests Russia's 'hypersonic' Kinzhal missile is powered by American tech – Sandbox

Artificial Intelligence: Stupidity is Dangerous

U.S. Made Components of Russian Weapons Systems found by Ukraine

- **Pantsir-S1 Air Defense System (AD)**
  - AMD
  - Rochester Electronics
  - Texas Instruments
  - Linear Technology

- **Kh-101 Cruise missile (~35 American made microchips)**
  - Atmel Corp
  - Cypress Semiconductor
  - Infineon Technologies
  - Intel
  - Maxim Integrated
  - Onsemi
  - Texas Instruments
  - Rochester Electronics
  - XILINX

- **Ka-52 Alligator (~22 American components)**
  - Altera USA
  - Analog Devices Inc.
  - Burr-Brown
  - Linear Technology
  - Micron Technology
  - TE Connectivity
  - Texas Instruments
  - Micro Technology

Where did the chips originate? **How were these components sourced?** Are these components not military-grade but still useful for military use? **Are these recycled components? Unregulated markets?** Were they taken out of dishwashers and refrigerators? **How old are they?**
Some were manufactured in 2020 and 2021 according to stamped date of manufacture
Do we have a breakdown or non-existent export control systems?

Note: There were components made in Austria, Canada, China, Germany, Japan, Netherlands, South Korea, Switzerland, Taiwan, the UK, and USA
(About 18% had an assigned Export Control Classification Number [ECCN])

Sources:
Jeanne Whalen. U.S. probing how American electronics wound up in Russian military gear. The Washington Post. 15 June 2022. FBI, Commerce agents probing American electronics in Russian military gear – The Washington Post
Zach Schonfeld. Hundreds of Western components found in Russian weapons in Ukraine: think tank. The Hill. 8 Aug 2022. Hundreds of Western components found in Russian weapons in Ukraine: think tank | The Hill

So What? What is the solution? A whole-of-Government approach to controlling the illegal export of American technology.

A Dysfunctional Relationship with China

The competition with China over the deployment of advanced weapons systems and weaponized AI is very complicated to explain and understand. In addition to dysfunctional export controls, PRC cyberhackers have been successful in stealing lots of American secrets. For example, between 2013 and April 2015, they hacked files from the Office of Personnel Management (OPM). Among the items stolen were millions of SF-86 security clearance forms, with personal information and fingerprints of people applying for a security clearance.[419] Personal data of an estimated 22 million current and former federal employees were compromised, including employees of the American intelligence agencies. Cases of Chinese espionage have been frequently detected by the U.S. intelligence community since 2000. Many Chinese expatriates have been charged with espionage.

> "The greatest long-term threat to our nation's information and intellectual property, and to our economic vitality, is the counterintelligence and economic espionage threat from China."
>
> **Christopher Wray**
> **Director, FBI**

Do Chinese weapons systems have American and other Western technology embedded in them? The Iranians and the Russians do, why would the Chinese Communists stay out of the game? Dysfunctional security systems are an open door to anybody who wants to take advantage of American *naïveté*. (Meaning lack of good judgment and wisdom.) There are examples in the open domain. For instance, a Chinese company called *Phytium Technology* uses American software and supercomputers to build knowledge of hypersonic vehicles, including missiles that someday could be fired at American military targets.[420] This company with known ties to the Chinese military has been on the U.S. Department of Commerce (USDOC) since at least 2015, but somehow, they can obtain American technology due to the dysfunctions in export control systems.

A renewed effort to stop the illegal export of American hi-tech components to China was announced in April 2021 by President Biden, to stop the flow of technology to dozens of Chinese companies, including three known

---

[419] Josh Fruhlinger. The OPM hack explained: Bad security practices meet China's Captain America. CSO Online. 12 February 2020. The OPM hack explained: Bad security practices meet China's Captain America | CSO Online

[420] China Builds Advanced Weapons Systems Using American Chip Technology. TechWebTrends.com. 8 April 2021. China Builds Advanced Weapons Systems Using American Chip Technology - TechWeb Trends

manufacturers of supercomputers for the military.[421] [422] In February 2023, the Biden Administration announced a new effort to stop American investments in China that result in the outflow of advanced technology, particularly in advanced computing and AI. Included in this new effort is an attempt to convince EU and NATO members to create parallel restrictions in and on the outflow funding and technology transfer to China. In part, these efforts resulted from the flight of a Chinese spy balloon across the U.S. which vividly documented the Chinese threat. The incident brought together Republicans and Democrats in Congress, to stop the adversarial Chinese actions.[423]

A Chinese Trojan Horse

Cranes operating at the Tampa (Florida) Port facilities. If they were made in China and had installed sensors and cameras, they could report military movements near CENTCOM and SOCOM. (Picture taken by The author.)

In March 2023, it was revealed that ship-to-shore cranes manufactured by ZPMC, a Chinese state-owned company that has been installed at practically all the leading American ports, were fitted with cameras and sensors that can transmit back to the PRC critical information on the movements of cargo, including military supplies and the movement of naval assets.[424] [425] Once again, Chinese espionage successfully exploits American vulnerabilities and gets away with it because there is an endemic lack of courage and audacity (gonads) to do something about it. ZPMC has about 70% of the global market for these cranes, which means that U.S. European allies have also been had, together with countries all over the world that have installed similar equipment. Are the Chinese clever or what?

Shanghai Zhenhua Heavy Industries Company Limited (ZPMC), is a PRC government-owned company, rated as the world's largest manufacturer of port

---

[421] BBC. US blacklists seven Chinese supercomputer groups. *BBC*. 9 April 2021. US blacklists seven Chinese supercomputer groups - BBC News

[422] Nicholas Eftimiades. The 5 Faces of Chinese Espionage: The World's First 'Digital Authoritarian State.' Braking Defense. 22 October 2020. The 5 Faces Of Chinese Espionage: The World's First 'Digital Authoritarian State' - Breaking Defense

[423] Ana Swanson and Lauren Hirsch. U.S. Aims to Curtail Technology Investment in China. *The New York times*. 9 February 2023. U.S. Aims to Curb Investment in China Amid Security Concerns - The New York Times (nytimes.com)

[424] C=Kristen Altus. Chinese 'spy cranes' part of the 'most comprehensive penetration' of US history: Gen Jack Keane. MSN. 7 March 2023. Chinese 'spy cranes' part of the 'most comprehensive penetration' of US in history: Gen. Jack Keane (msn.com)

[425] John Feng. China Accuses U.S. of Paranoia Over Spy Cranes Concerns. Newsweek. 6 March 2023. China Accuses U.S. of Paranoia Over Spy Cranes Concern (newsweek.com)

cranes to handle containers, and is present in at least 36 of 166 countries. [426] In addition to sending special crews to install the cranes, handle maintenance with teams of Chinese workers that are dispatched all over the world. The. U.S. provides them special temporary visas to enter the country and maintain the cranes at all critical supply-chain ports.[427] It took some time, but the FBI found the espionage equipment at the Port of Baltimore as far back as 2021.[428] For whatever it is worth, no American companies are producing similar cranes, which makes the U.S. practically hostage to this type of espionage. There are only a couple of more expensive European crane manufacturers in existence, and they have been losing market share to the cheaper Chinese alternative. Chinese spy agencies have outdone the possibly metaphorical Greek Trojan horse told in the Aeneid by the Roman poet Virgil who wrote about it in 29 B.C. Chinese spies are within the American battlements already. This is not an ancient legend or a metaphor. This situation goes beyond computer malware, deceptive computer codes, and the weaponization of AI, but without a doubt, advanced surveillance software is part of this scheme to gather sensitive information.

The Chinese Spy Balloon

On 2 February 2023, NBC News reported that a Chinese spy balloon had entered U.S. airspace, and was flying over the country collecting sensitive national security information.[429] After days of news media speculation about the capabilities of the balloon, it was finally revealed that China could control the balloon to make multiple passes over military sites, collect, and transmit signals intelligence, to China in real-time. For days, as the balloon travelled across the country, the news media and government spokesmen and elected officials speculated about the capabilities of the balloon, the capability of national security agencies to disrupt or block the signals, and the best way to shoot it down without causing potential damage or casualties if it was shot down before it went out to sea. The entire episode was mishandled. From 28 January to 4 February 2023, when it was finally shot down, China many have collected lots

---

[426] 上海振华重工(集团)股份有限公司

[427] Check the ZPMC USA website: Who we are (zpmcusa.com).

[428] Justin Cooper. Chinese cranes can spy on US ports, be taken over, officials warn American Military News. 6 March 2023. Chinese cranes can spy on US ports, be taken over, officials warn (americanmilitarynews.com)

[429] Courtney Kube and Carol E. Lee. Chinese spy balloon gathered intelligence from sensitive U.S. military sites, despite U.S. efforts to block it. NBC. 3 April 2023. Chinese spy balloon gathered intelligence from sensitive U.S. military sites, despite U.S. efforts to block it (nbcnews.com)

of sensitive information to enhance its database of U.S. national security information, which in the age of AI, is the key to gaining supremacy. The debris was recovered, and the equipment reconstructed, but once again national security was put at risk.[430] Other similar airships have been spotted flying over Latin American countries collecting information, allegedly for civilian use. All of these surveillance and data collection is another piece of the competition for supremacy on AI, which is dependent on a huge database of all kinds of information. So now what? How long has this been going on? Senior Pentagon officials have acknowledged that this was not the first time U.S. airspace was violated, but information on previous instances is classified.[431] [432] [433] The new term currently in use to describe these balloons is *unidentified anomalous phenomena* (UAPS).

Alibaba, Baidu, Huawei, TikTok, Tencent, Xiaomi, ZTE, and others

An increasing number of Chinese IT companies are becoming leaders in the global social media market. They have become metaphorical digital Trojan Horses. These popular Chinese companies have Chinese Communist Party representatives on site, and are an extension of their intelligence agencies. Without a doubt, they are using these popular software companies to mine data and influence public opinion, and behavior. They have the ability to sway young people away from traditional beliefs, and create bias for multiple purposes. Of critical importance is the ability to mine data, and increase the size of Chinese '*mega data*' by extracting large amounts of information for nefarious purposes from unsuspecting users. The U.S. Government has launched multiple probes into how these Chinese IT companies operate, but the process to ban their access to the U.S. market to mitigate national security risks is very slow. (This is not a fictional story or comedy.)

The Chinese PLA has used multiple outlets provided by leading Chinese software companies to hack military-linked information, as well as a huge amount of personal data of Americans, including Social Security numbers,

---

[430] Paul LeBlanc. Everything you need to know about the suspected Chinese spy balloon. CNN. 6 February 2023. What you need to know about the suspected Chinese spy balloon | CNN Politics
[431] Meredith Deliso. Chinese spy balloon timeline: Where it was spotted before being shot down. *ABC News*. 5 February 2023. Chinese spy balloon timeline: Where it was spotted before being shot down - ABC News (go.com)
[432] Katherine Tangalakis. The 3 Chinese spy balloons spotted during the Trump administration were initially classified as UFOs. *Business Insider*. 6 February 2023. The 3 Chinese spy balloons spotted during the Trump administration were initially classified as UFOs (msn.com)
[433] Erin Banco. What the Biden administration isn't telling Congress about spy balloons. *Politico*. 21 March 2023. What the Biden administration isn't telling Congress about spy balloons - POLITICO

addresses, birth dates, credit card information, and other personal data.[434] [435] The U.S. Federal Communications Commission (FCC) has officially designated Huawei and ZTE as national security threats.[436] A ban on the purchase and use of equipment and services provided by both companies is in effect for U.S. Government entities, because they are suspected of being used for espionage. Both companies have also been banned from purchasing semiconductors and other American high-tech products. Other countries, including Australia, Japan, and the UK have put in place similar bans on the products and services of these Chinese companies. All companies in China are required to cooperate with the PRC government's intelligence agencies, including having a representative of the Chinese Communist Party embedded in their staff. Other Chinese companies affected by similar bans by the FCC include Hytera Communications, Hangzhou Hikvision Digital Technology, and Dahua Technology.[437]

The Chinese search engine Baidu Inc. has been listed as a potential security risk and malicious actor. Investigators determined that when the Baidu web browser is used by Microsoft Windows and Android platforms, it sends personal data to company servers, including the location of the user through GPS, URLs visited, and other personal data. One interesting detail is that not only the Chinese, but also intelligence organizations from Australia, Canada, New Zealand, the UK, and the U.S. have taken advantage of vulnerabilities in the Baidu browser to extract information about users. The Baidu browser was found to be transmitting unencrypted and easily decryptable user information to Baidu servers, which allow for the data to be collected by outside parties, including intelligence agencies and cybercriminals. [438]

The FBI has openly stated that Chinese intelligence activities present a significant threat to the national security of the U.S. Chinese spy agencies have repeatedly hacked U.S. Government agencies, and stolen a large volume of military secrets and personal data of individuals who work or have worked for

---

[434] Zach Dorfman. Tech Giants are Giving China a Vital Edge in Espionage. Foreign Policy. 23 December 2020. How China's Tech Giants Like Alibaba, Tencent, and Baidu Aid Spy Agencies (foreignpolicy.com)

[435] Alexandra Alper. Exclusive: U.S. examining Alibaba's cloud unit for national security risks- sources. Reuters. 19 January 2022. Exclusive: U.S. examining Alibaba's cloud unit for national security risks - sources | Reuters

[436] Arjun Kharpal. China's Huawei and ZTE were officially designated 'national security threats' by the FCC. CNBC. 30 June 2020. FCC: Huawei and ZTE officially designated 'national security threats' (cnbc.com)

[437] US labels five Chinese tech firms as security risks. DW. 13 March 2021. US labels five Chinese tech firms security risks – DW – 03/13/2021

[438] Jeffrey Knockel Sarah McKune, and Adam Senft. Baidu's and Don'ts: Privacy and Security Issues in Baidu Browser. Munk School, University of Toronto. 23 February 2016. Baidu's and Don'ts: Privacy and Security Issues in Baidu Browser - The Citizen Lab

government agencies, including the 16 members of the U.S. intelligence community.⁴³⁹ Every bit of stolen data forms part of a puzzle that can be put together by China to overtake the U.S.'s role as the global leader in AI.

Monster from Ancient Chinese Tale
Contemporaneous Chinese IT monsters
Are Very Real

Source: Library of Congress

---

⁴³⁹ Carnegie Endowment for International Peace. Limiting Chinese National Security Espionage. Carnegie Endowment for International Peace. 25 April 2022. Limiting Chinese National Security Espionage - U.S.-China Technological "Decoupling": A Strategy and Policy Framework - Carnegie Endowment for International Peace

Theft of American Intellectual Property

> *"It takes something more than intelligence to act intelligently."*
> *Fyodor Dostoyevsky*

Chinese theft of American intellectual property has been going on uninterrupted for over fifty years, starting before President Richard Nixon's historic visit to China in February 1972. The visit, without a doubt, changed the course of history. But the U.S. did not gain a new ally. Bold moves do not necessarily produce desired effects. A new and growing military superpower and an economic competitor were born. *Annual losses to China due to intellectual property theft have been estimated to top $360 to $600 billion annually!* [440] The DHS and the FBI have warned repeatedly about Chinese IP theft using traditional methods, such as espionage, as well as hacking. Stealing American technology and trade secrets is a favorite Chinese pastime.[441] What was regarded as a victory by undermining the Soviet Union during the Cold War, turned out in the long run to have contained serious unintended effects. Despite the frequency of the subject in news media headlines, and a lot of talk about it by elected officials, very little if anything has been done about it.[442]

Cybercriminals Weaponizing AI

There are many complex cyber-security challenges, as outlined earlier. *Are there dark forces out there that have the technology to cripple the U.S. electric power grid system? Do they have killer satellites that could destroy our intelligence collection systems? Can they concoct sophisticated deepfakes that can mislead our defensive hi-tech systems?* The answer is clearly yes. This assortment of

---

[440] Sherisse Pham. How much has the US lost from China's IP thefts? CNN. 23 March 2018. How much has the US lost from China's intellectual property theft? (cnn.com) anticipate these events, and the government obtained a profit. However, the Reagan Administration had the 'brilliant idea' of privatizing these events.

[440] BBC. US blacklists seven Chinese supercomputer groups. *BBC*. 9 April 2021. US blacklists seven Chinese supercomputer groups - BBC News

[440] Nicholas Eftimiades. The 5 Faces of Chinese Espionage: The World's First 'Digital Authoritarian State.' Braking Defense. 22 October 2020. The 5 Faces of Chinese Espionage: The World's First 'Digital Authoritarian State' - Breaking Defense

[440] Sherisse Pham. How much has the US lost from China's IP thefts? *CNN*. 23 March 2018. How much has the US lost from China's intellectual property theft? (cnn.com)

[441] Masood Farivar. US Intensifies Crackdown on China Intellectual Property theft. *Voice of America*. US Intensifies Crackdown on China Intellectual Property Theft (voanews.com)

[442] Perhaps Americans need to paint the White House blue in hope of electing a baby boy with the courage to do something about the problem.

criminal elements has direct and indirect ties to Russian and China's intelligence organizations. Further collaboration of these dark forces could further undermine U.S. and ally security by coordinating and expanding hacking. The expansion of an alliance of international cybercriminals is not far from materializing. There are already signs that a new alliance of dark forces is forming.[443] [444] The link between cybercriminals targeting private and public institutions globally and rogue states is self-evident. Where are most ransomware attacks originating? Ransomware is resulting in losses of over $20 billion annually, and are expected to increase to over $265 by 2031. Most attacks are originating in Russia, Iran, China, and North Korea. Controlling the Internet is practically impossible.

Leaks of Classified Information

AI cannot protect against evil spirits and stupidity. National security secrets are being stolen and leaked into social media, causing untold damage to the safety of the nation, relationships with key allies, and collective defense agreements. The ability of the state to protect and defend the citizenry is torpedoed every time that national secrets are spilled. In the *Age of AI*, illegal disclosure of classified documents is suicidal. At least 300 pictures of classified documents were leaked sometime between January and March 2023, and members of the IC are baffled because it took so long to discover the leak. However, once the FBI and other members of the IC focused on the problem, it did not take very long to figure out what happened. As has been pointed out, the key to leadership in AI is to have the top database in the world. Any and all leaks cause damage to the challenge of maintaining a supremacy in stored information of all types.[445]

Jack Teixeira
Source: Instagram

In early March 2023, and possibly as far back as January 2023, over 100 '*Secret/NoForn*' documents appeared in social media, spread through *Discord*,

---

[443] Christopher Burgess. Russia-China cybercriminal collaboration could 'destabilize" international order. CSO United States. 28 June 2022. Russia-China cybercriminal collaboration could "destabilize" international order | CSO Online

[444] Damien Black. Cybercrime from Russia and China: what can we expect next. *Cybernews*. 24 January 2023. Cybercrime from Russia and China: what can we expect next? | Cybernews

[445] Shane Harris and Samuel Oakford. Discord member details how documents leaked from closed chat group. *The Washington Post*. 12 April 2023. Discord member details how documents leaked from closed chat group - The Washington Post

Twitter, 4chan, Telegram, and other social media and gaming sites.[446] The leak was first reported by *The New York Times on 7 April 2023*.[447] The information leak did not make the headlines until early April. After a few days of speculation, *The Washington Post* claimed that it had been traced to the leader of a group of '*gamers*' employed at a military base, who went by the nickname OG. Finally, on 13 April, the FBI arrested Airman 1st Class Jack Teixeira, a 21-year-old '*Cyber Transport System*' specialist, and member of the Massachusetts Air National Guard, assigned to the 102nd intelligence Wing.[448]

There are no vaccines against stupidity, which has more strains that COVID 19. Guidelines for handling and protecting national security were violated in multiple ways, and the systems in place failed to detect the leak for at least three months. This is a classic case of closing the barn door after the horse escaped! How a stupid low-rank airman got access to very sensitive classified information and was able to make copies and sneak out Top Secret//NOFRN documents is an undeniable example of mismanagement and quantum stupidity.

The authenticity of the documents circulating on the Internet has not been established, as Russian intelligence may have tinkered with them to disseminate false information related to the invasion of Ukraine. The documents showed typical markings of the Defense Intelligence Agency (DIA), National Geospatial-Intelligence Agency (NGIC), the National Security Agency (NSA), and the Bureau of Intelligence and Research of the Department of State (DOS).[449] The leaked documents include assessments of how the Russian military has been impacted by serious loses in Ukraine, as well as how the Russian intelligence establishment has been penetrated, and how Ukraine has benefitted from critical intelligence information provided to them by NATO members. The documents

---

[446] Olga Robinson, Shayan Sardarizadeh, Jake Horton. Pentagon Leak: How secret files on Ukraine spread, then disappeared. BBC. 10 April 2023. Pentagon leak: How secret files on Ukraine spread, then disappeared - BBC News

[447] New Batch of Classified Documents Appears on Social Media Sites. *The New York Times*. 7 April 2023. New Leak of Classified Documents on Social Media Alarms Pentagon - The New York Times (nytimes.com)

[448] Greg Norman, David Spunt, Liz Friden, Gillian Turner, Jake Gibson, and aul Best. FBI arrests Massachusetts Air National Guardsman Jack Teixeira in probe f classified leaks. Fox News. 13 April 2023. FBI arrests Massachusetts Air National Guardsmen Jack Teixeira in probe of classified document leaks (msn.com)

[449] Yaroslav Trofimov and Nancy A. Youssef. Pentagon Investigates More Social-Media Posts Purporting to Include Secret. U.S. Documents. *The Wall Street Journal*. 7 April 2023. Pentagon Investigates More Social-Media Posts Purporting to Include Secret U.S. Documents – WSJ

Artificial Intelligence

provide assessments of the losses suffered from Ukraine and how dependent they are on receiving help from the U.S. and other NATO partners.[450]

The leaked documents could be part of a disinformation campaign. But whose psychological operation? Who could be trying to confuse who? According to some analysts in public media, as well as Ukrainian President Zelensky, claimed that the documents are fakes. As a well-established historical policy, the U.S. Intelligence Community (IC) does not comment on any released classified documents, particularly about their authenticity.[451] [452] [453] *Why did the intelligence community depart from a long-standing policy of not commenting on spilled classified documents?*[454] There are more questions than answers, but this new episode in a series of leaks of sensitive information indicates that it is time that the *Espionage Act* be applied to the full extent of the law. In the age of AI, in hindsight, people like John Walker, Robert Hanssen, Aldridge Ames, Harold James Nicholson, Jonathan Pollard, Clayton J. Lonetree, Chelsea Manning, Edward Snowden, Henry Kyle Freese, Ana Montes, Carlos and Elsa Alvarez, should have been given the same treatment given to Ethel and Julius Rosenberg in 1953.[455] [456]

---

[450] DNYUZ. Leaked Documents Reveal Depth of U.S. Spy Efforts and Russia's Military Struggles. DNYUZ. 8 April 2023. Leaked Documents Reveal Depth of U.S. Spy Efforts and Russia's Military Struggles – DNyuz

[451] James Bickerton. Leaked U.S. Documents Spark Fear in Russian Pro-0War Blogging Community: ISW. *Newsweek*. 8 April 2023. Leaked U.S. Documents Spark Fear in Russian Pro-War Blogging Community: ISW (msn.com)

[452] Ukrainska Pravda. Leak of US Documents exposes Russians' fear of a Ukrainian counteroffensive – ISW. *Ukrainska Pravda*. 7 April 2023. Leak of US documents exposes Russians' fear of a Ukrainian counteroffensive – ISW (msn.com)

[453] Shane Harris and Dan Lamothe. Intelligence leak exposes U.S. spying on adversaries and allies. The Washington Post. 8 April 2023. Intelligence leak exposes U.S. spying on adversaries and allies (msn.com)

[454] Bernd Debusmann Jr. Pentagon documents leak a risk to US national security, officials say. BBC. 10 April 2023. Pentagon documents leak a risk to US national security, officials say - BBC News

[455] Tim Ott. Julius and Ethel Rosenberg: Their Case, Trial and Death. *Biography*. 25 March 2020. Julius and Ethel Rosenberg: Their Case, Trial and Death (biography.com)

[456] Julius and Ethel a(Greenglass) Rosenberg were members of the Communists Party of the United States of America (CPUSA) and spies for the Soviet Union. They were brought to trial on 6 March 1951, under the Espionage Act of 1917. They were executed in the electric chair at the Sing Sing Prison in New York.

A History of Misreading the Tealeaves

> **It is not the strongest of the species that survive, not the most intelligent, but the one most responsive to change.**
>
> **Charles Darwin**

AI, feeding versatile robots and intelligent machines may be effective, but they may not necessarily work any better than humans that write the algorithms that move them. There were plenty of warning signs and missed signals before the terrorist attacks of September 11, 2001.[457][458][459] However, all the lights blinking red were missed by humans in the intelligence community (IC). Muslim extremists, led by al-Qaeda, had declared a Jihad (war) against the U.S. An affinity group had carried out an attack using a truck bomb against the World Trade Center in New York City in 1993. Two U.S. embassies had been bombed in August 1996, in Kenya and Tanzania. The USS Cole had been targeted by two suicide terrorists in Yemen on 12 October 2000. By May 2001, the CIA's counterterrorism center had information that something was cooking, and there were indications that the U.S. was going to be hit hard by a transcendental and uncanny terrorist attack.[460] The CIA warned the White House a day before the attack that there were many indications that something was about to happen, but despite all the warnings, human intelligence failed to uncover and stop the attacks before they happened, and 2,977 people died. More have died since then, particularly the first respondents in New York City from toxins swirling among the wreckage.

After 9/11/2001, President George W. Bush and the U.S. Congress created the bipartisan *'National Commission of Terrorist Attacks Upon the United States,'* on 27 November 2002. The Commission concluded that the CIA and the FBI had inadequately assessed the threat posed by al-Qaeda. And had failed to take action to disrupt the terrorist planning. AI is without a doubt a *'transformative'* technology, but it does not necessarily replace the decision-making process that humans engage in before decisions are made. AI-driven autonomous weapons systems may or may not work for the purpose they were

---

[457] CNN. September 11 Warning Signs Fast Facts. *CNN.* 29 August 2022. September 11 Warning Signs Fast Facts | CNN

[458] Patrick Jackson. September 11 attacks: What happened on 9/11? *BBC.* 3 August 2021. September 11 attacks: What happened on 9/11? - BBC News

[459] Barbara Maranzani. How U.S. Intelligence Misjudged the Growing Threat Behind 9/11/ History.com. Updated 11 September 2018. How U.S. Intelligence Misjudged the Growing Threat Behind 9/11 – HISTORY

[460] Chis Whipple. What the CIA Knew before 0/11: New details. *Politico.* 13 November 2015. What the CIA knew before 9/11: New details – POLITICO

designed. Machines may be versatile but do not necessarily work any better than humans. Humans make mistakes, and machines empowered by AI can also make mistakes. Robotic weapons systems do not necessarily work better than human brains that create them. Robotic *'thinking'* may not deliver a miraculous cure to wanton stupidity, boneheadedness, and brainlessness among so-called *'intelligence analysts.'*

To start with, weaponized AI, particularly autonomous physical weaponry, has limitations, and could make serious errors of *'judgment.'* It is entirely possible that these weaponized AI systems could be fooled, and reprogrammed by cyber criminals and state-sponsored rogue actors. Behind the scenes, the old-fashion cat-and-mouse intrigue in the world of intelligence is always competing for supremacy. There are all kinds of feeds going into AI-linked databanks and information systems, and the results that can be obtained by weaponized AI always depend on the quality of the data. Although the development of autonomous weapons systems is progressing rapidly, there are plenty of dark forces in the game. Who has the better algorithms, the best data, the superior microchips, and the outstanding skilled AI engineers? The complex algorithmic systems behind weaponized AI are the key to success in cyberwarfare.[461] [462]

Reading of tea leaves for fortune-telling - *tasseography or tasseomancy* - has been around for several centuries, and may have originated in China, or possibly in the Scottish Highlands. Spooky spiritualism, exotic mysticism? Not less accurate than misreading intelligence signs of trouble ahead.

---

[461] Jayshree Pandya. The Weaponization of Artificial Intelligence. Forbes. 14 January 2019. The Weaponization Of Artificial Intelligence (forbes.com)

[462] Mark Minevich. How to combat the Dark Side of AI. Forbes. 28 February 2020. How To Combat The Dark Side Of AI (forbes.com)

AI and American Society

A new era of AI has emerged, but it is too early to assess what the results will be. Without a doubt, personal privacy is a thing of the past. AI algorithms can mix good and false information, including details of a person's political or religious viewpoints, which could result in discrimination, worker layoffs, a reduction in manual labor jobs, or in the creation of better paying jobs. There is a wide range of opinion regarding positive and negative outcomes. In general, the public is not informed about what is taking place in high-tech labs, and as a result, there is very little opportunity for public opinion to guide the results. Media pundits espouse all kinds of nonsense, while suffering from profound ignorance about AI, and without taking responsibility for their limited knowledge and commentary. Without a doubt, the national security of the U.S. would be in considerable danger if American technology is overtaken by competing countries that have the stated goal of reaching military supremacy.

National defense planning is more complex than AI algorithms. There is a lot of activity taking place behind a wall of silence that is only occasionally opened to the public. For example, on 15 March 2023, it was reported that the U.S. Air Force hypersonic Scramjet missile was tested successfully. This hypersonic airbreathing weapon concept (HAWC) has been in development for some time, together with other weapons systems and planes that can reach Mach 5 speeds. Sure, the Russians and Chinese have been flaunting their experiments with hypersonic weapons, but that is part of their *braggadocio* political system. They like to project an image of increasing power in order to retain power by confusing their populations.

The U.S. Defense Advanced Research Projects Agency (DARPA) is not prone to the same bombast and fanfaronades as China and Russia. For example, there are at least two hypersonic missile systems, including the AGM-183A air-launched Rapid Response Weapon, which have been successfully launched from a B-52H. The *Skunk Works'* operations with companies like Lockheed Martin are real.[463] [464] Another example of the increasing sophistication of American weapons systems is the deployment of the U.S. Air Force 6th-generation stealth fighter, and 'loyal wingman' droves, called Combat Collaborative Aircraft (CCA). Drones that can be controlled from the air by other aircraft instead of ground

---

[463] Darren Orf. The Air Force's Hypersonic Scramjet Missile Aced Its Final Test, beautifully. MSN News. 15 March 2023. The Air Force's Hypersonic Scramjet Missile Aced Its Final Test, beautifully (msn.com)

[464] Sascha Brodsky. It Sure Seems Like Darkstar, Lockeed's Secret High-Speed Jet, Is Real. 15 March 2023. It Sure Seems Like Darkstar, Lockheed's Secret High-Speed Jet, Is Real (msn.com)

stations, increase the processing of time-sensitive data and reduce the sensor-to-shooter time. The U.S. Navy is working behind the scenes to upgrade naval air power. For example, a 6th-Generation F/A-xx carrier-launched stealth fighter is being developed. For obvious reasons, secrecy has to be maintained to keep predators away, and not much may be made public until the 2030s.[465] Through the use of advanced AI algorithms managing multiple sensors and mission systems, American air power continues to be a global leader.[466] AI and Quantum Computing are behind all of these developments. One cannot happen without the other. Although time after time and with increasing frequency incidents happen that indicate that Americans are dumb and stupid, that is not necessarily the case.

---

[465] Kris Osborn. The U.S. Navy is Developing F/A-XX: The Key to Air Supremacy? *MSN*. 16 March 2023. The U.S. Navy is Developing F/A-XX: The Key to Air Supremacy? (msn.com)

[466] Kris Osborn. NGAD Is Born: The Air Force's 6th Gen Stealth Fighter is Already Flying. 15 March 2023. NGAD Is Born: The Air Force's 6th Gen Stealth Fighter is Already Flying (msn.com)

Conclusions / So What?

There is nothing permanent except Change.

Heraclitus

AI is not science fiction, but a new reality that changes everything. AI is developing rapidly and not about to be paused for any type of safety measures. All areas of human activity are vulnerable and AI presents a threat to humanity itself. The U.S. is assessed as the global leader, but nobody knows who is the *'top dog,'* because a lot of the action is kept in deep secrecy. AI is not an antidote for lack of common sense, sloppiness, carelessness, and poor judgment. Just because the U.S. is ahead today, it does not follow that the situation cannot change overnight. Despite lots of speculation, there is no confirmation of any instance in which a robot killed anyone in combat without human participation. Not yet, but it could happen before this book comes out of the print shop. Anything is possible in the new world *'disorder.'*

For all practical purposes, personal privacy has been lost to AI-linked technology that collects, processes, and shares all forms of biometric and financial data with other entities, both private and public. Social media is *a warzone*, now enhanced by AI. All kinds of nefarious actors use AI to trick victims out of their money using very creative ways to confuse and take advantage of people. Multiple forms of cyberattacks, including DDoS, ransomware, social engineering, hacking, spear phishing, whaling, and fake news distribution, are powered by weaponized AI. AI is data-centric. Social media platforms are exploited by embedding false information to take advantage of a wide range of human vulnerabilities for criminal purposes.

In the arsenal of intelligence and counterintelligence operations, the *'art of deception and counter deception'* have been enhanced with the use of AI. Weaponized AI has been used to disseminate *'Deepfake'* disinformation, generate fringe ideological discourse, and cause multiple disruptions. Espionage and intelligence gathering have been around since ancient times and will continue magnified, strengthened, supplemented, and intensified by technological developments, such as AI.

The weaponization of AI is advancing, and is well on its way to changing all forms of warfare in the physical and cyber worlds. The weaponization of AI is *'inescapable,'* i.e., cannot be avoided or denied. Under the concept of *hybrid warfare*, AI-supported weapons systems can target military personnel, equipment, facilities, information systems, infrastructure, supply chains, and anything and everything critical and vulnerable *'without ethical considerations.'* The best way to mitigate against the weaponization of AI is to be ahead of a diverse collection of rogue actors and develop countermeasures against a vast array of physical, cyber, and scientific threats. Mitigation can only be achieved through the use of superior weaponized defensive AI systems. The future of warfare is dependent on speed based on weaponized AI – Making quick and accurate decisions based on a huge amount of data – and with weapons that can fire with a certain amount of autonomy from human interaction.

The key players in weaponizing AI are the U.S., China, Russia, the UK, France, Israel, and South Korea. Chinese Communist leaders have made AI a national strategic priority for the PRC, as they position themselves to become dominant across the board, and they are making progress every day. Although the U.S. is the leading power in the world, and the leader in weaponized AI, the situation is not static. In the world of AI, control of illegal technology exports is critical. The U.S. and its allies cannot afford to operate dysfunctional export controls. American intelligence has to be expertly managed and protected against domestic and foreign enemies, as well as stupid people. There is no known vaccine against stupidity, which has more strains than the COVID-19 virus. As Russian President Vladimir Putin clearly stated in 2017, "*Whoever reaches a breakthrough in developing artificial intelligence will come to dominate the world.*"

Appropriate Biblical Commentary for the Challenges of AI

Ecclesiastes 10:1
Dead flies can make a whole bottle of perfume stink, and *a little stupidity can cancel out the greatest wisdom.*

Proverbs 16:22
Wisdom is a fountain of life to the wise, but *trying to educate stupid people is a waste of time.*

Proverbs 1:32
Inexperienced people die because they reject wisdom. *Stupid people are destroyed by their own lack of concern.*

Proverbs 14:33
Wisdom is in every thought of intelligent people; *fools know nothing about wisdom.*

Ecclesiastes 2:13
Oh, I know, "Wisdom is better than foolishness, just as light is better than darkness.

Proverbs 4:6
Do not abandon wisdom, and she will protect you; love her, and she will keep you safe.

Proverbs 9:12
You are the one who will profit if you have wisdom, and if you reject it, you are the one who will suffer.

Proverbs 10:23
It is foolish to enjoy doing wrong. *Intelligent people take pleasure in wisdom.*

Proverbs 16:16
It is better—much better—to have wisdom and knowledge than gold and silver.

INDEX

This Index was generated by software. It is created based on the way names appear on the manuscript in alpha-numerical order. Thus, people are listed as they appear in the text by their first name instead of their last name.

'CHIPS and Science Act', 30
144th Guards Motor Rifle Division, 124
4th Industrial Revolution, 11, 51
Abto Software, 118
academic institutions, 24
Academy of Military Medical Sciences, 38
Academy Smart, 118
Acer, 30
Acropolium, 118
actionable insight's, 19
Adam Osborne, 25
Admiral Charles Richard, 98
affinity credit card', 58
Agility Robotics, 83
Agiliway, 118
AGM-183A air-launched Rapid Response Weapon, 150
AI weapons, 11, 13, 95, 103, 108, 112
AI weapons systems, 11, 13, 95, 108
Air Line Pilots Association, 82
airlines, 57, 58, 59, 61
Aitheon, 116, 118
Alaska, 22
Albert Einstein, 136
Aldridge Ames, 147
Aleksandr Zhukov, 74
Alexa, 15, 48
algorithmic warfare, 13
algorithms, 33, 49, 55, 60, 81, 84
Algorithms, 33, 49, 108
Alibaba, 97, 141, 142
Alphabet Inc., 14
al-Qaeda, 148
Al-Qaeda, 45
AMAI, 127
Amazon, 15, 48
Amazon Web Services, Inc., 14
American technology, 99, 122

Ana Montes, 147
André Mignot Hospital, 72
Android, 50
Angels IT, 127
anomalies, 19
Antal Russia, 127
Anti-aircraft missile system Stugna-P, 115
Apple Inc., 14
Apri.group, 127
Apriorit, 118
Arab-Israeli war of 1973, 22
Archer Software, 118
Argentina, 72
Armata T-14 Main Battle Tank, 103
Arsmoon, 118
Artezio, 127
Artificial Intelligence, 1, 8, 11, 13, 15, 16, 19, 39, 43, 51, 85, 86, 90, 91, 94, 95, 97, 103, 105, 112
Assistant, 15, 48
Atomic Creative, 127
Attack UAV helicopter RZ-500, 114
attitudinal data, 24, 44
Augmented Pixels, Inc, 116
Australia, 74, 142
Australian Strategic Policy Institute, 130
authenticators, 35, 36
AutoCAD, 120
autonomous vehicles, 15
autonomous weapons systems, 94, 129, 130, 131, 148, 149
avionics, 100
Azure, 48
Baidu, 97
Baidu Inc., 142
Baidu Translate, 50
Baidu, Inc., 14
banks, 8, 57, 60, 91

Bayraktar TB2, 112
behavioral data, 24, 44
Bell Labs, 48
Best Business-Out-Of- Business, 118
Biden Administration, 43
bioinformatics, 38
biological dominance, 38
bio-medical research, 38
biometric authentication, 35, 49
biometrics, 15, 34, 35, 36, 37, 60, 62, 91, 112
biotechnology, 38
Bitcoin, 72
Black Basta, 73
Black Cat, 70
Boston Dynamics, 83
brain-computer interfaces, 63
brainwaves, 63
Broadcom, 30, 31
BroutonLab, 127
Bulgaria, 74
Bureau of Intelligence and Research, 146
Bureau of Mines, 22, 23
Burning Buttons LLC, 127
Business-Automatics, 118
ByteDance, 43, 97
California, 22, 29, 30, 116
Canada, 74, 142
Canonical Group, 83
carelessness, 8, 122, 152
Carlos and Elsa Alvarez, 147
Central Military Commission, 97
Centre Hospitalier Sud Francilien, 72
Chatbots, 118
ChatGPT, 53, 54, 55, 81
CHI Software, 118
Chief of the General Staff of the Russian Armed Forces, 124
child pornography, 13
China, 8, 13, 38, 45, 47, 50, 51, 60, 95, 96, 97, 98, 99, 100, 103, 104, 153
Chinese college and university students, 99
Chinese Communist Party, 44, 142
Chinese espionage, 99
Chinese Government, 43, 50, 51, 99
Chinese intercontinental ballistic missiles, 98, 99
Chinese Spy Balloon, 140

CHIPS and Science Act of 2022, 131
CIA, 92, 148
Cisco, 120
Cisco Systems Inc., 14
Clausewitz, 92
Clayton J. Lonetree, 147
Clever Data, 127
Cloudflare, 120
Clover Dynamics, 118
CMCC, 73
CodeInside, 127
Cold War, 41, 87
Combat Collaborative Aircraft, 150
common sense, 122, 123
Competence, 127
computer age, 17
computer chips, 28, 29, 30, 31
Computer Science, 33, 83
computer sciences, 99
Computers, 24
Congressman Jake Auchincloss, 54
Conti, 70
conventional military equipment, 108
Cortana, 15, 48
Costa Rica, 70
counter-deception, 13, 89, 152
counterintelligence, 8, 13, 62, 89, 152
COVID, 29, 30, 39, 61, 99, 117
COVID pandemic, 99
COVID-19, 61
Crimea, 107, 124
criminal enterprises, 13
Critical infrastructure, 51
cruise companies, 8, 57
CryWiper, 73
Customs and Immigration, 61
CVisionLab, 127
Cyber espionage, 100
cyber hygiene, 46, 47
Cyber Transport System, 146
Cybercrime, 13
cybercriminals, 69, 70, 72, 90
Cybercriminals, 52
cybersecurity, 44, 45, 51, 65
cyberspace, 51
Dahua Technology, 142
Dallas, 31
DarkLime, 118

DARPA, 48, 150
Dasha.ai, 127
Data, 17, 19, 24, 37, 44, 57, 61, 62, 105, 115
Data integration, 17
data points, 68, 84
Data Pro Software, 118
Data Science UA, 118
Data validation, 17
DataRoots Labs, 118
DB2 Limited, 118
deception, 8, 11, 13, 46, 47, 89, 91, 152
Deception, 46, 47, 89, 90
deepfakes, 89, 90
Defense Advanced Research Projects Agency, 48, 150
Defense Intelligence Agency, 99
Dell, 30
Denver, 70
Department of Defense, 17, 21, 51, 97, 106
Department of State, 146
Department of Transportation, 21
destructive behaviors, 46
Devanthrop, 83
Developex, 118
Devrain, 118
Digital Design, 127
Disinformation, 45
DNA, 34, 35, 36
DOD, 17, 18, 36, 41, 44, 51, 60, 97
DOE, 22, 23
Doomsday Clock, 87
DopplePaymer, 73
Douyin, 97
Drones, 150
Duke University, 63
Dyson, 83
Eastern Europe, 70
EAvergreen, 118
EBO, 21, 22
Edvantis, 118
Edward Snowden, 147
Effective, 127
Effects Based Operations, 21
EIA, 22, 23
electromyography, 63
Elon Musk, 53
Embrox Solutions, 118
Empat, 118

ENBISYS, 127
Endurance, 73
engagement data, 24, 44
engagement patterns, 34
ENIAC, 24
EPSON, 25
ESTESIS Technologies, 127
Ethel and Julius Rosenberg, 147
Evrone, 127
Exadel, 118
Exciting reality, 127
Expert Committee on the Development of Artificial Intelligence, 116
extended warranty scams, 52
extortion, 69
Facebook, 41, 42, 45, 90
Facebook Inc., 14
facial images, 15
facial patterns, 33
Facial Recognition Technology, 60
factual information, 24, 44
fake news, 13, 14, 90, 152
false rumors, 45
Fang Guoyu, 96
FBI, 8, 46, 47, 70, 71, 72, 73, 75, 140, 142, 144, 145, 146, 148
Federal Aviation Administration, 21, 82
Federal Protective Service, 75
Federal Security Service, 75
fembots, 83
Fembots, 82
FGM-148 Javelin, 109
FIM-92 Stinger, 109
FIN7, 73
financial institutions, 8, 57, 58
fingerprint records, 91
fingerprints, 33, 34, 36
Finland, 13
First Line Software, 127
Flyaps, 118
Ford, 15
Foreign Intelligence Service, 75
Forest Valley, 127
Fortifier, 118
France, 72, 95, 113, 153
Franklin D. Roosevelt, 85
frequent flyer programs', 59
FTC, 30

future of warfare, 13, 153
gait, 34
General Electric, 14
General Sergei Shoigu, 123
Generative AI, 81
Geosplit, 127
Germany, 13, 29, 110, 113
Giant Leap Lab, 118
GIS systems, 120
GitLab, 118
Global Foundries, 29
GM, 15
Go Wombat, 118
Google, 15, 33, 48, 49, 50, 51, 52, 53, 55, 68, 81, 120
Google Translate, 15, 49, 50, 51
Google Voice, 52, 53
Government employees, 36
GPTZero, 55
Greeks, 89
gynoids, 83
Gynoids, 82
hacking, 12, 14, 36, 45, 90, 95, 152
hand geometry, 36
handwriting, 34
Hangzhou, 142
Harold James Nicholson, 147
Heather Roff, 90
Hewlett-Packard, 31
Hikvision Digital, 142
HIMARS launchers, 123
Honda Motors, 83
Honeycomb Software, 118
Hoomano, 83
hotel chains, 57
HP, 30
Huawei, 31
Huayiwang Translation, 50
human biology, 38
human features, 33
human genes, 95
HumanIT, 118
Humanoids, 82
Humans, 15, 19, 86
Hunter RSVK-M2 Unmanned Ground Vehicles, 115
Husky Jam, 127
hybrid warfare, 13, 152

hypersonic Scramjet, 150
hypersonics, 100
Hytera Communications, 142
IA, 16
IBM, 14, 29, 48, 120
Idealogic, 118
Igor Girkin, 122
Iliad, 89
imitate human behavior, 43
India, 83, 128, 130
i-Neti, 127
information systems, 13, 51, 152
Inoxoft, 118
INSART, 118
Insilico Medicine, 127
Instagram, 41, 42
Integrio Systems, 118
Intel, 14, 29, 92
intellectual property, 30, 99
Intellica, 118
Intelligence, 13, 15, 16, 43, 46, 47, 62, 85, 86, 90, 95, 97, 103, 105, 112
Intelligent automation, 16
Intent Solutions Group, 118
Interstate Oil & Gas Compact Commission, 23
Intspirit, 127
Intuitive Robots, 83
ISIS, 45
ISS Art, 127
IT Test, 127
Italian, 17
Italy, 70
Iteora GmbH, 127
Iterative.ai, 127
iTranslate, 50
ITRex Group, 118
J.D. Power, 59
Jack Teixeira, 146
Japan, 142
Jappware, 118
Jazzros, 118
Jean Dixon, 85
Jessica Livingston, 53
JetSoftPro, 118
Jinn-Bot Robotics, 83
John Walker, 147
Jonathan Pollard, 147

Kamikaze drone ST-35 "Thunder", 113
kamikazidrones, 108
Kazan Higher Tank Command School, 124
killer robots, 12
Kindred Systems, 83
Kyiv, 116
Lapsus, 72
laptops, 24, 50
lasers, 29
LATECO, 127
Law enforcement, 13
Leju, 83
Lemberg Solutions, 118
Lenovo, 30
linear regression, 84
LineUp, 127
Litslink, 118
Louisiana, 22
Lt. Gen. Robert P. Ashley, 99
Lucid Reality Labs, 118
Luggage tags, 61
M-55S tanks, 109
Macco Robotics, 83
Machiavelli, 92
MadAppGang, 118
Magnise, 118
Main Intelligence Directorate, 75
Major General Ding Xiangrong, 97
Makiivka, 123
MANPADS, 109
Massachusetts Air National Guard, 146
mathematical modeling, 84
Maze, 73
Mercedes-Benz, 15
Merriam-Webster Dictionary, 12, 15, 19, 89
Meta Platforms Inc., 14
microchips, 28
Micron, 30
Micron Technology, Inc, 14
Microsoft, 14, 15, 48, 50, 52, 53, 55, 68, 81, 116, 120, 124
Microsoft Corporation, 14
Microsoft Translator, 50
military superiority, 8, 12
military tacticians, 91
Mindware, 73
Ministry of Digital Transformation, 116

MIT, 18, 39, 63, 106, 119
Mlvch, 127
Mohajer-6, 135
money laundering, 13
Morphological biometrics, 34
Moscow Institute of Physics and Technologies, 105
Musically, 43
myTHE, 127
Napoleon IT, 127
NASA, 21, 82, 116
National Academy of Sciences, 116
National Cyber Strategy, 51
National Geospatial-Intelligence Agency, 92, 146
National Security Agency, 65, 73, 92, 146
NATO, 110, 113, 119, 120, 122, 126, 139, 146
natural language processing, 48
navigation patterns, 34
NBC News, 140
NCSC, 8, 46, 47
nefarious actors, 8, 12, 36, 45, 62, 152
Neurobotics, 127
New Mexico, 22
New Zealand, 74, 142
North Dakota, 22
Nostradamus, 86
Ntechlab, 127
NTR Labs, 127
Nuance Communications, 48
Nvidia, 30, 72
NVIDIA, 14, 72
Office of Personnel Management, 36
Oklahoma City, 23
OpenAI, 53, 55
Open-Source Enterprise, 92
open-source intelligence, 91, 112
Operational Net Assessment, 22
Optimum-web, 118
Oracle, 14, 43, 120
organic intelligence, 12
Osage Nation, 23
OSINT, 91, 92
Oxford Dictionary, 85
PAL Robotics, 83
Palo Alto, 116
patterns of life, 60, 62
patterns of typing, 34

Pennsylvania, 23
People.ai, 118
People's Drone PD-1 / PD-2, 114
personal privacy, 57, 61
Peter Thiel, 53
Pew Research Center, 45
phishing, 69, 72
photographs, 34
physical movements, 34
PLA Daily, 96
political scientists, 91
poor judgement, 8, 122, 152
Postindustria, 118
predictive analytics, 38, 61, 84
predictive modeling, 19, 84
Preply, 118
President Barack Obama, 130
President Donald J. Trump, 131
President Jimmy Carter, 22
problem solving, 8, 11, 15
Proffiz, 118
Promobot LLC, 127
Prostir, 118
psychologists, 91
PSYGIG, Inc., 83
QBMT, 83
QStudio.org, 127
Qualcomm, 30
Quantum, 118
Quantum Computing, 27, 28, 151
Raas, 73
RAND Corporation, 18
ransomware, 14, 90, 152
Ransomware, 69, 70
Raspberry Robin, 73
React AI, 83
RefaceAI, 118
Reid Hoffman, 53
Relevant Software, 118
Requestum, 118
Reuters, 38, 43, 123
REvil, 72
Richard Nixon, 85
Rinf.tech, 118
Roasted Ox Leg, 127
Robert Hanssen, 147
Robotic weapons systems, 12
robotics, 100, 103

Robotis, 83
Rocket Harbor, 118
Rockwell Automation Inc., 14
rogue actors, 12, 152
Roman Valeryevich Seleznev, 74
Roonyx, 127
Rubius, 127
Russia, 8, 13, 45, 47, 90, 95, 103, 104, 105, 107, 108, 109, 111, 112, 119, 120, 122, 123, 153
Russian, 13, 17, 90, 95, 96, 103, 104, 107, 108, 109, 110, 112, 115, 119, 120, 122, 153
Russian commanders, 112, 122, 123
Russian military barracks, 123
Russian military equipment, 108, 109, 122
Russian Minister of Defense, 123
Russian Navy, 103
Russian sloppiness, 123
RZ-500 attack drone, 114
Sam Altman, 53
Samsun Group, 14
Samsung Electronics, 29
San Diego, 30
San Jose, 30
Sannacode, 118
Santa, Clara, 29
SAP SE, 14
Sberbank, 104
Scalamandra, 118
science fiction, 1, 8, 12, 24
scientific modelling, 124
Secretary of Defense of Robert McNamara, 17
security breaches, 36, 45, 47
Self-learning, 12
semiconductor, 28, 29, 30, 31, 72
Senate Homeland Security and Governmental Affairs Committee, 43
Seoul, 29
Shadow Robot Company, 83
Shahed-131, 135
Shahed-136, 135
Shanghai Zhenhua Heavy Industries Company, 139
Shoebox machine, 48
Siemens AG, 14
Simlabs Inc, 127
Singapore, 29, 130

Singularika, 118
Siri, 48
Skunk Works, 150
SkyGuru, 127
Sloboda Studio, 118
sloppiness, 8, 122, 152
smart cell phones, 24
Sobolsoft, 50
social engineering, 14, 152
Social media, 8, 41, 44, 45, 46, 84, 152
Softgroup, 118
Softjourn, 118
SoftMediaLab LLC, 127
Solutions, 118
Solvve, 118
SourceX, 118
South Korea, 14, 29, 83, 95, 130, 153
Soviet Union, 107, 147
Spamouflage Dragon, 46
Spanish, 17
SPD, 118
spear phishing, 14, 152
speech recognition systems, 48
Speech-to-text, 48
Spirit DSP, 127
S-PRO, 118
ST-35 Silent Thunder loitering munition drone, 114
Su-57 5th generation multi-role fighter jet, 103
Supercomputing, 38
Surveillance, and Reconnaissance, 105
Sweden, 112, 130
Switchblade, 113
Symphony Solutions, 118
Systems, 12, 14, 20, 21, 51, 72
Systems theory', 20
T-72, 109
T-90M, 108
tactical advantage, 11, 94
Taiwan Semiconductor Manufacturing Company, 29
Tallium Inc, 118
Team Harbor, 118
Technaxis, 127
Techprostudio, 118
Temy, 118
Tencent, 97

Tesla, 15, 64, 68, 82, 83, 129
Texas, 22, 30, 31
Texas Instruments, 30, 31
The APP Solutions, 118
THeMIS UGVs, 113
Thucydides, 92
Tieto, 127
TikTok, 43, 44, 56, 97, 141
TIQUM, 127
Touch-screen kiosks, 60
Toyota Motor, 83
TraceAir, 127
Traces.AI, 118
transistors, 28
TrendLine Global, 118
Trojan Horses, 43
Trojans, 89
troll farm, 90
True engineering, 127
Trump Administration, 43
Twitter, 41, 42, 46, 90
U.S., 11, 12, 34, 35, 36, 37, 43, 45, 46, 47, 48, 51, 57, 62, 86, 90, 95, 96, 97, 103, 104, 105, 109, 112, 113, 153
U.S. Armed Forces, 99
U.S. Department of Commerce, 138
U.S. Department of Energy, 22, 51
U.S. DOD, 130
U.S. Federal Trade Commission, 30
U.S. Members of Congress, 30
U.S. Navy, 151
U.S. Securities and Exchange Commission, 30
U.S.-Israel Artificial Intelligence Center, 55
Ubiquitous surveillance, 61, 62
Ubtech, 83
Uinno, 118
UK, 11, 13, 30, 73, 83, 90, 95, 110, 112, 113, 124, 126, 130, 133, 142, 153
Ukraine, 13, 29, 30, 74, 86, 87, 95, 96, 98, 103, 104, 105, 106, 107, 108, 109, 110, 111, 112, 113, 114, 115, 116, 117, 118, 119, 120, 121, 122, 123, 124, 125, 126, 128, 135, 136, 146
Ukrainian defenders, 122
Ukrainian intelligence, 123
Ukrainian military, 109, 112, 113, 114, 115
Ukrainian President Zelensky, 147

University of Minnesota, 54
Unmanned aerial vehicles, 112
US National Institute of Standards and Technology, 60
USJFCOM, 21, 22
UVL Robotics, 127
Valery Gerasimov, 105, 123
VALL-e, 52
Visioneer, 48
Vitaliy Goncharuk, 107, 116
Vladimir Putin, 13, 86, 104, 107, 112, 153
Vladislav Klyushin, 74
Walmart, 43
Washington Monument, 86
Watson, 48
WayRay, 127
weapon, 11, 51, 60, 89, 94, 96, 109, 113, 114
Weaponization of AI, 13
weaponized virus, 19
Weapons, 12, 94, 95, 103, 104, 122
weapons systems, 12, 13, 24, 95, 105, 113, 122, 152
WebbyLab, 118
Webdevelop PRO, 118
Webiomed, 127
West Virginia, 23
Western literary tradition, 89
whaling, 14, 152
Whiz Kids, 17, 18
WikiLeaks, 90
Windows, 48
Wollow, 127
Working Geeks, 127
WWII, 11, 24, 48, 95
Xentaurs, 127
Yahoo, 30, 33, 53, 81
Yandex, 119, 127
Yellow, 118
Yotalabs, 118
ZeBrains, 127
Zen, 127
Zenbot, 127
zettabytes, 19, 24, 44
Zfort Group, 118
Zhenbao Island, 104
ZPMC, 139
ZTE, 142
ZuZex, 127
ZYFR, 127

www.ingramcontent.com/pod-product-compliance
Lightning Source LLC
LaVergne TN
LVHW020413070526
838199LV00054B/3593